Advance Applause

Most books on the market tell parents what they have done wrong in raising their kids. Phil Callaway's approach is REFRESHINGLY DIFFERENT.... He tells what his parents did *right*. I'm sure you will find this and his warm storytelling style a real treat!

—Bob DeMoss
Youth Culture Specialist
Focus on the Family

Out of the constellation of family books, the work of Phil Callaway is A SPARKLING STAR. His writing is crisp, his humor is fresh, and his points hit home. This is a book you'll love.

—Max Lucado
Author of *No Wonder They Call Him
the Savior, He Still Moves Stones,* and
When God Whispers Your Name

Put this book on your MUST-READ LIST. You'll love Phil Callaway's contagious humor and down-to-earth wisdom.

—Kathy Peel
Contributing editor of
Family Circle magazine

Phil Callaway has discovered the key ingredients to a healthy family life—lots of love, lots of faith, and loads of laughter. He packs a double portion of all three in his new book, *Daddy, I Blew Up the Shed.*

—Martha Bolton
Bob Hope staff writer and author of
Honey, The Carpet Needs Weeding

RICH WISDOM gleaned from pulling on some deep veins in the ordinary rock of a life of faith.

—John Fischer
Author of *St. Ben* and *Real
Christians Don't Dance*

Very few authors make me laugh out loud. Phil Callaway makes me ROAR. Maybe that's why I savor his books like a cup of hot chocolate. Sipping each story slowly, rolling it around my mouth to get the full flavor, then spitting it all over the room in reaction to the hilarious truth. Ready to enjoy yourself? Then open your heart, grab your sides, and read *Daddy, I Blew Up the Shed.*

—Ken Davis
Author, comedian,
motivational speaker, Daddy

With his usual REFRESHING style, Phil Callaway CELEBRATES the humor, joy, and grace abounding in the ordinary, and the mysterious miracles made possible through faith in Christ, right in the midst of the mundane.

—Ellen Santilli Vaughn
Writer and coauthor, with Chuck Colson, of *The Body*

In *Daddy, I Blew Up the Shed,* Phil Callaway regales the reader with tales of youth and family life, packed with pleasantries worthy of a Mark Twain. Unlike Twain, however, he also conveys Christian principles in a gentle, unobtrusive manner—never preachy, always apt. Here is reading for GREAT FUN—and GREAT VALUES.

—Paul L. Maier
Author of *A Skeleton in God's Closet* and *Pontius Pilate*

Are you tired of bad news and hungry for some good?... Do you love TALES OF THE UNEXPECTED told by writers who leave out the parts readers skip? Then *Daddy, I Blew Up the Shed* is for you. Phil Callaway is Dave Barry with a message. I sprained my wrist turning pages.

—Joel Freeman
Author of *God Is Not Fair* and chaplain of the NBA Washington Bullets

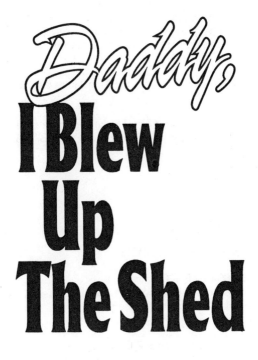

Daddy, I Blew Up The Shed

Phil Callaway

HARVEST HOUSE PUBLISHERS
Eugene, Oregon 97402

Except where otherwise indicated, all Scripture quotations in this book are taken from the Holy Bible, New International Version®, Copyright © 1973, 1978, 1984 by the International Bible Society. Used by permission of Zondervan Publishing House. The "NIV" and "New International Version" trademarks are registered in the United States Patent and Trademark Office by International Bible Society.

Verses marked KJV are taken from the King James Version of the Bible.

Some of the stories in *Daddy, I Blew Up the Shed* have appeared in a different form in *Servant* magazine, a ministry of Prairie Bible Institute, Three Hills, Alberta, Canada.

DADDY, I BLEW UP THE SHED

Copyright © 1994 by Phil Callaway
Illustration Copyright © by John McPherson
Published by Harvest House Publishers
Eugene, Oregon 97402

Library of Congress Cataloging-in-Publication Data

Callaway, Phil, 1961–
    Daddy, I blew up the shed / Phil Callaway.
        p.   cm.
    ISBN 1-56507-244-8
    1. Family—Religious life. 2. Christian life—Humor. 3. Family—
United States—Humor. 4. Family—United States—Anecdotes.
5. Christian life—Anecdotes. 6. Callaway, Phil, 1961– I. Title.
BV4526.2.C23   1994
248.4—dc20   94-11501
                                                                  CIP

94 95 96 97 98 99 00 — 12 11 10 9 8 7 6 5 4 3 2 1

Dedication

*For one whose shy smile on an August evening
launched the adventure of a lifetime.
For the heart in my home; the sparkle in my eyes;
the Honey in my books.
For you, Ramona.*

Thanks

Stephen, Rachael, and Jeffrey: Because of you I shall never experience writer's block. Thanks...I think. Thanks, too, for teaching me as much about God as I've taught you. May none of us forget what we're learning.

Mom and Dad: For 51 years of commitment—a legacy of faithfulness that will outlive us all.

Vance and Sherri, Larry and Julie: With friends like you, who needs babysitters?

Paul and Judy, Dave and Linda, Kevin and Ivy: For long-distance friendships strengthened by the fact that you've not called collect. Yet.

My schoolteachers: For sending me out of classrooms, putting me in corners, and keeping me after school. I needed the time to work on my jokes.

John McPherson: You are wonderfully warped. Keep it up.

My co-workers at Prairie Bible Institute: Your encouragement has made this fun. Your prayers have made it a joy. Keep shaping lives to change this old world.

My friends at Harvest House...

> *Bob Hawkins, Jr.:* For laughing in that restaurant.
>
> *Eileen Mason:* For taking a big-time chance on a small-town boy.
>
> *Teresa and Janna:* For grinning when my face came through the fax machine. Knowing you found humor in the situation has helped in the healing process.

My Savior, Jesus Christ: For crowning the last two difficult years with Your joyful presence. For allowing me a small role in Your story. And most of all, for providing the hope of eternity—with family.

Contents

Author's Note

The only names which have been changed are those of the innocent.

From the Start

When I was born I was so shocked that I didn't say a thing for more than a year. Once I was able to speak I desperately wanted to write about the experience, so I spit out my soother and asked Mom for a word processor. It was her turn to be shocked. "Hey," she said, before plugging me back in, "this is 1962. They haven't been invented yet."

At the ripe old age of five I penned my first book. It was entitled *Five More Minutes* and the plot turned upon the antics of a small boy who asked his mother if he could stay out for a few extra innings of baseball. When she said yes, he got so excited that he slid head-first into third. Third was a swing set. The boy was taken to a hospital. The boy was me.

That was pretty much all I wrote because, for the life of me, I couldn't think of a moral to the story. Don't ask permission? Don't obey your mother? Don't slide head first? I published the book anyway—minus a moral—and it enjoyed a limited circulation due to the fact that our dog Inky ate the only copy.

Last year all that changed. My first real book, *Honey, I Dunked the Kids*, was released by a real publishing company, and some humans liked it. One of them approached me to say that it had been of great help in his home. "It helped us balance out our television set," was how he put it. "Well," I replied, blushing slightly, "that's good to hear. I was hoping to encourage parents to shut off the tube and spend more time with their kids."

"No, that's not what I meant," he said kindly. "Ever since we bought little Theodore a jackknife, the front leg on the left side has been wobbly. We needed something about half an inch thick. Your book was perfect."

A lady from Kansas wrote to accuse me of spying on her family and writing stories about them. "I swear *yoi* have been staying at our *hoise*," she wrote, after confessing that one of her "angels" had spilled Pepsi on her typewriter, giving it "a mind of its *oin*."

Then there was the frightening phone call—a frenzied wife seeking counsel: "My husband is dying of laughter right here at our kitchen table." There was panic in her voice. "This is the first time in a long while that I've seen him laugh. Should I be grateful or dial 911?" Of course, I told her to be grateful.

The most satisfying report came from a lady who went to visit her 85-year-old mother in the hospital. As she approached her room one Friday afternoon, she heard strange noises. Upon entering, she found her mother surrounded by the customary monitors, plastic tubes, get-well cards, and a bed pan—but today she was laughing herself silly. On Monday she went to be with the Lord.

Years ago, a ten-year-old walked into the lingerie department of a clothing store. He bashfully told the clerk that he wanted to buy a slip for his mom. "What size is she?" asked the clerk. "I dunno," said the boy. The lady explained that it would be helpful if he could describe her—was she fat, thin, short, tall? "Well," the boy replied, "she's just about perfect." So the clerk sent him home with a size 34. The following Monday his mother returned to exchange the gift. It was a little tight. She needed a size 52. According to her boy, however, she was just about perfect.

I'm a little like the kid in the lingerie section. On occasion I'm accused of sizing things up wrong. Of painting overly optimistic pictures of family life. Of laughing in the face of heart monitors and get-well cards. After all, say the critics, the family is in rough shape. Look at the statistics. And, of course, they are right. But frankly, I'm tired of hearing how badly parents have messed up our world. I'm weary of the media's portrayal of the family. Of a television that shows no respect. Of sitcoms with laugh tracks in all the wrong places. There is a part of me that says, "Hey, Roseanne Barr, you've had your day in the shade. We would like to hear some *good* news for a change. We would like to hear about families where strange and hilarious things occurred and children didn't have to spend the rest of their lives recovering from them. We would like to hear about parents who fell...and got back up. About children who sinned...and found forgiveness."

That's what this book is all about. If you read between the laughter, you'll hear the voice of a man who can't thank God enough for his childhood. For a mom who spanked his bottom. A dad who tickled his toes. For siblings who made him rich by offering him cash to play elsewhere. You'll also hear the voice of a father who can't thank God enough for his family. For kids who light up like Christmas when Daddy walks through the door. For a wife who still finds him attractive when his hair is blowing in the breeze and he hasn't the energy to chase after it.

I should issue a warning, though: If you sent your ten-year-old to the bookstore to pick up a copy of the latest *Surefire Formula for Forging the Perfect Family*, and he came back with this one, you may want to exchange it. But if you believe life is too serious not to laugh, and if you enjoy grinning at your reflection in the pages of another family, then I think this book will fit you just right.

—Phil Callaway
Three Hills,
Alberta, Canada

1
Three Spankings and a Funeral

MIDTERM TODAY!

$F=MA$
$S=\frac{1}{2}AT^2$
$A=\pi r^2$

McPHERSON

KNOWING THAT HE'D BE SITTING BEHIND BRIAN, ED SNUCK INTO BRIAN'S LOCKER DURING GYM CLASS AND WROTE SEVERAL CRUCIAL FORMULAS ON THE BACK OF HIS SHIRT.

"

Having adventures comes naturally to some people. You just have a gift for them or you haven't.

—Anne of Green Gables

Mercy imitates God and disappoints Satan.

—St. John Chrysostom

Don't carry a grudge. While you're carrying the grudge the other guy's out dancing.

—Buddy Hackett

He who cannot forgive others breaks the bridge over which he must pass himself.

—George Herbert

My father was a Methodist and believed in the laying on of hands.

—A.W. Tozer

"

If I could relive any of my school years, I'd pick grade five in a minute. This was the year the new teacher came to town to spend her rookie year conducting experiments in our classroom. Her name was Miss Ida Weissmuller and we had trouble pronouncing it. In fact, we made up other names as substitutes. They felt better in our mouths, but I wouldn't even whisper them now.

In September, she assigned me a spot behind Bobby Spaulding, who laughed at my jokes, and across the aisle from a weepy girl with horn-rimmed spectacles and a name I can't recall. By February, Miss Weissmuller had drilled us well in the essentials of penmanship and English protocol. By March she had strapped me soundly more than once— three times, to be precise—and in so doing, enabled me to claim an enviable school record which stands unchallenged to this day.

It is not the sort of record you boast about when you have school-aged children of your own, nor was it the sort kept in office cabinets. But we students had a filing system of our own. My first trip there was the direct result of a joke which I whispered into Bobby's ear during mathematics. I don't remember the punch line right now and it is just as well because it was not the sort of thing you boast about when you are older and more mature. Bobby thought it quite funny, though, judging from the way he laughed himself into a slouch and made a slow recovery.

"Perhaps you would like to stand and share with the rest of the class what is so funny, *Ja?*" said Miss Weissmuller, her thick German accent pushing mathematics even further from everyone's mind. Bobby tried his best to obey, but once upon his feet, he couldn't utter a single word. He just stood there bent in half, one hand clutching his stomach, the other pointing at me.

As you may have guessed, this was not my first offense that day and I was sent to the principal's office for six strong lashes with a leather strap that was a good deal thicker than my hands.

I developed a fond dislike for that strap, and I did not care for Miss Weissmuller either. She was too strict—I felt—and her hair was always in a bun drawn too tight to allow her much smiling. I pointed these things out to my mother one evening and received a clear message: "She's your teacher, Philip. You may not like her but she has been put there for a purpose and we will find out what that purpose is." I wasn't quite sure what she meant, but I knew that her sentiments were not shared by all the parents.

In mid-March, one mother stormed angrily into the classroom and removed her son—books, pencils, and all. He never returned. Moved clean out of the district, some said. We students watched with interest as the dust settled and, strangely, found ourselves siding with Miss Weissmuller. For the next few days we listened to her every word, refrained from joke-telling, and kept quiet without being told. But such things come to an end, and for me the ending was high in drama.

"Put your books away, *Ja,*" said Miss Weissmuller. "It's

time for our Bible memory test." The words struck horror
into my ten-year-old heart. Once a month we wrote out
verses from the Bible and our marks were clearly reflected in
our report cards. My marks had been slipping ever since first
grade, and this month they were destined to slip further. I
had been too busy with lesser things to store away Scripture.
So I slid some verse cards from my desk, lodged them on the
chair between my legs, smiled saint-like at the weepy girl
across the aisle, and in desperation, began to cheat on my
Bible verses.

Believe it or not, this is what I wrote: "My little children,
these things write I unto you, that ye sin not. And if any man
sin, we have an advocate with the Father, Jesus Christ the
righteous: And he is the propitiation for our sins: and not for
ours only, but also for the sins of the whole world" (KJV).

At this point I folded my hands, looked quizzically toward
the blackboard, and continued to write: "And hereby we do
know that we know him, if we keep his commandments. He
that saith, I know him, and keepeth not his commandments,
is a liar, and the truth is not in him. But whoso keepeth his
word, in him verily is the love of God perfected." I even
wrote out the reference correctly: "1 John 2:1-5."

Sleep was slow in coming that night. Oh, my report card
would be looking better, but in the darkness tidy report cards
don't hold a candle to clean consciences. *You are a liar, Phil,
and the truth is not in you.* Quietly I made my way into my
parents' bedroom. Without a word I climbed between their
sheets.

"What's wrong?" asked Mom.

"Nothin'," I replied.

"It's almost midnight, son," she reminded me. "What's
the matter?"

I spoke in muffled tones: "Mom...I...um...cheated-
onatest."

"You what?"

"I...um...well...I cheated on my memory verses."

We talked some more and then we prayed, asking God's forgiveness. I was leaving the room a lot lighter when Mom stopped me in my tracks: "You'll have to tell Miss Weissmuller, too."

I didn't sleep much that night for thinking about the punishment. It would be administered in the schoolyard, probably in the heat of afternoon recess. Ministers from the surrounding area gather, wearing black suits and solemn expressions. The mayor is there. He introduces Miss Ida Weissmuller's speech and all the schoolchildren listen attentively to her: "We are gathered here today to witness the conclusion of an awful blight on each one of our reputations, *Ja.*" The younger children strain their necks to get a good look at me. The older ones simply nod their agreement and look away. Bobby, too. Miss Weissmuller isn't finished, though: "Today I have learned that Philip Ronald Callaway cheated on his Bible memory verses." A collective gasp arises. The girl from across the aisle removes her horn-rimmed spectacles and dabs the corners of her eyes. Miss Weissmuller continues with little emotion: "Let each of us resolve to conduct ourselves in an obedient and orderly fashion, with sobriety and prudence, lest we end up like this poor young man—this . . . this . . . *cheater.*" The children then file by me in a solemn procession, from the youngest to the eldest. Each is handed a stick that they toss, with a sigh, around the swing set leg to which I am tied. Then the ministers strike matches and toss them on the sticks. Emotionless, Miss Weissmuller fans the flames. With my report card.

The small graveside service held the following Tuesday is attended by my parents only. My sister and brothers are too ashamed to come. They study algebra instead. *"He cheated on his Bible memory verses,"* they remind each other in hushed tones. But years later they sneak into the graveyard late one night, their flashlights searching out my tiny tombstone engraved with these words:

THE UNKNOWN STUDENT
1961–1971

**For habits he would not break
He was ceremoniously burned
at the stake
His sins are too many to list
He certainly will not be missed.**

May *we* rest in peace.

No, I did not sleep well that night.

The next morning I crept bleary-eyed into the school building. Early. The other students weren't there yet, but Miss Weissmuller was. She waited inside the courtroom, gavel in hand. I tapped on the door. "Come in," said a thick accent. I opened the door obediently. She sat behind her desk, dressed mostly in black. My judge. My jury. My executioner.

"May I help you?"

I forced myself forward and stood still before her. "I came to tell you that... I'm sorry," I said, unable to look up. "I... um... cheated on Bible memory yesterday."

"And how did you cheat, Philip?"

"I copied off the verse cards."

"Did anyone see you?"

"I don't think so."

"Did *God* see you?"

I looked up for the first time. "Yes," I said. "He kept me awake last night."

Tiny traces of a smile formed around her eyes. "Then you've asked His forgiveness, *Ja?*"

"Yes."

She smiled widely in spite of the bun in her hair. "I forgive you, too," she said. "After school today you will take the test over."

From that day onward, I didn't cheat on another test. Oh, I was accused of it once in high school. But I didn't do it.

You are a liar, and the truth is not in you.
Yes. But God forgave me.
You cheated on Bible memory.
Yes. But I told Miss Weissmuller. And she forgave me, too.

If I could relive any of my school years, I'd pick grade five in a minute.

————

We are like men when we judge,
like God when we forgive.

2

Of Records Broken and Promises Kept

" ———————————————————————

If I had known my son was going to be president of Bolivia, I would have taught him to read and write.

—Enrique Penaranda's
mother

I have difficulty praying the Lord's Prayer because whenever I say, "Our Father" I think of my own father, who was hard, unyielding and relentless. I cannot help but think of God that way.

—Martin Luther

Parents are the bones on which children sharpen their teeth.

—Peter Ustinov

The law tells me how crooked I am. Grace comes along and straightens me out.

—Dwight Lyman Moody

——————————————————————— **"**

One of the first things that attracted me to my wife was her incredible ability in the kitchen. When we were first going out (to this day I'm not sure where we were going, but that's what we called it), I remember listening to her prepare a snack. I was straining my ears for a sound with which I had grown up. Then, sure enough, there it was: *Whoops!* followed a split second later by a distinctly familiar crashing sound. *Ah,* I thought, *this is the woman for me. She is just like my mother.*

You see, my mother used to break things around our house. In fact, she wasn't content to break one dish. She would break entire sets. *Whoops!* Mother didn't stop at dishes, though. She broke eggs. Spanking spoons. Beatles records. But during those years, one thing seemed to remain intact: her word. If Mom said she would do something, she did it. Her words were commandments, etched in stone, but not always heeded. "You talk like that again, son, and I'll wash your mouth out with soap." I can't recall the word or why I deemed its usage necessary, but 30 years later I can still taste the soap. New and improved Dove. If I'm outside when the memory comes along, I look around me, then I spit twice.

Mom did not limit herself to soap, however. She kept the cupboard stocked high with cayenne pepper. "You sing that again and you'll burn for it," she told my brother Tim, who had taken to revising some of her favorite hymns and teaching them to his impressionable little brother:

> My hope is built on nothing less
> Than Scofield's notes and Scripture Press.
> I dare not trust the Word alone
> 'Cuz I can't read it on my own.

I had no idea what a Scofield was, nor a cayenne for that matter, but I was destined to taste one of them. As Tim stood defiantly on the sofa, I joined him in the glad refrain:

> On top of Old Smokey all covered with sand,
> I shot my poor teacher with a red rubber band.
> I shot her with pleasure, I shot her with pride.
> How could I miss her? She's 60 feet wide.*

To this day I despise cayenne pepper. You put it in a casserole and I can smell it driving by your house at 60 miles per hour with my windows rolled up. Mom seemed to like it, though. She piled it high on spoon handles, then inched it slowly in the direction of our tightly sealed mouths. Tim cleared his sinuses, *hmufff,* and the dread pepper cascaded to the floor in glorious rainbows of red. We laughed . . . until Mom stacked the hot stuff higher.

I took up running that day. A kid can only handle so much, you know, so I took off across a field, wondering what would happen if I just kept going and wasn't heard from again. "Kid missing, police follow hot trail," would make a good headline.

---

* In case you think my mother's punishment too harsh, it should be noted that we were singing another less printable version at the time.

OFFICER ONE: "Frank, I think I may have something here."
OFFICER TWO: "What is it, Biff?"
OFFICER ONE (sniffing his hand): "It's a trail of tiny red particles... smells like some sorta pepper."

Instead of being a statistic, however, I chose to be a tattletale, showing up at a friend's house and telling on my Mom. "She WHAT?" he said, amazement crossing his eyes.

"Ya, and it was hotter than the dickens."

"My Momma wouldn't do that." He slowly shook his head. "What's a dicken?"

Upon my arrival home later that afternoon, Mom told me most emphatically not to leave the yard again without asking permission. "Or," she said, "I will... uh... put you on a leash and tie you to the clothesline." The next day I ignored her warning and ran away again. When I returned Mom was waiting, like Charleton Heston, stone tablets in hand. And this is true: She placed Inky's red collar about my neck, clipped it to the leash, and swung me out to dry.

When I told this to my seven-year-old recently, he asked with wide eyes, "Were your feet touching the ground?"

"Yes, but barely," I replied. "That's why I'm so tall." Actually, I told him the truth: I sat on our back step, thoroughly enjoying myself. I had never seen the world quite this way before.

Like turtles, neighbor ladies poked their heads out windows. "That Bernice Callaway has gone too far this time," they said, shaking their necks. "She's gone clean over the edge."

Hey, I thought, sitting up straight. *I ran away, okay? I disobeyed. I'm getting what I deserve.*

They weren't so sure.

When I remind Mom of the incident, she winces a little. And when I tell others of my being collared, I get mixed reactions. Most laugh. But some sound like the turtles in our neighborhood. "The child was abused," they say behind their hands. "One of these days he'll just up and start barking uncontrollably."

But there is one reason they are wrong. There is one reason I don't have to battle past scars to tell of my childhood. It is simply this: The same hands that spanked me, held me. The same voice that spoke doom and gloom often whispered, "I love you." And I never once doubted that the whisper was true. After all, my mother may have broken some things, but she kept her word.

———

When love is remembered much is forgotten.

"

The three stages of a man's life:
1. *He believes in Santa Claus.*
2. *He doesn't believe in Santa Claus.*
3. *He is Santa Claus.*

Christmas, my child, is love in action.
—Dale Evans Rogers

I feel exactly as you do about the horrid commercial racket they have made out of Christmas. I send no cards and give no presents except to children.

—C.S. Lewis in a letter
to a friend

God's gifts put man's best dreams to shame.
—Elizabeth Barrett
Browning

"

Soft voices wake me this cold December morning. "Is it time yet, Dad? Is it time?" Outside our darkened window a white quilt blankets the ground. Inside three excited children are pulling at my covers, hopping on bare feet, and calling through the darkness: "Come on, Dad, come on."

Ah, yes. Now I remember. It is Christmas day. It is also ridiculously early.

Down the hall we go, coming to a halt before five stockings, concealing delectable and forbidden treasures.

"What about we eat 'em?" Jeffrey is three and speaks for the others.

"Not yet," I reply. "Wait 'til Mommy wakes up" and, "Ssshhh."

We plug in the Christmas tree lights then sit quietly on the couch. And while the world sleeps I tell them a tale from my childhood. A tale of Christmas past, largely true, and translated here for grownups. . . .

———

Once a year we children searched the skies for Grandpa. He always touched down during the Christmas season, so we would wait in the airport, our noses pressed against the frozen glass in painful anticipation. Then, sure enough, the silver bird would appear, cutting through the clouds just for us.

Our tradition at this point was to behave much like primates seeking bananas. And with good reason: Grandpa always brought a gallon of genuine maple syrup and a brown leather suitcase heavy with brightly wrapped packages (mostly for my sister).

We loved Grandpa for other reasons, too. For one thing, he was the only one I knew who drank cough syrup straight from the bottle, oblivious to its high alcoholic content. And you couldn't help but admire his head, too. It was as smooth as polished brass—only it grew less hair. My brother Tim claimed the barber merely put a stainless steel bowl over Grandpa's head one day and said, "That will be $1.50," but whatever the case, we couldn't get enough of running our hands over it and gazing at our reflections.

We also admired Grandpa's size. He was . . . well . . . a big man, poundage-wise. Grandpa Callaway could never be found far from a box of chocolates, and the years had charged him for it. There were definite advantages to Grandpa's girth, however. It was perfect to hide behind during certain games we played. Perhaps best of all, the five of us could find room on his lap simultaneously to hear the Christmas story year after year.

But this Christmas, it looked like Grandpa's plane had arrived without him. This was cause for concern, particularly for us young ones who couldn't help but wonder where maple syrup went which didn't come down. Of course, we weren't concerned only with the maple syrup. No, we were far more sensitive than that. We wondered where the presents were. So we waited and we watched. Other grandpas arrived to the hugs and kisses of kids like us. But not Grandpa Callaway.

Then Dad noticed someone off to one side. Could it be? He was the right size. He had the right face. But he also had hair. "GRANDPA!" we yelled.

"What in the wor...?" said Dad.

"A wig..." said Mom, her hand over her mouth, "...sort of."

Moments later a restroom mirror told Grandpa why he had escaped our notice. The wig was a good one. Expensive gray with streaks of black. But it was on sideways, the black streaking sideways, and the Made in Canada tag sloping neatly over his left ear. "Oh say," said Grandpa, over and over. "Oh say."

But the news would not get better. Grandpa's luggage, it seemed, had not made the journey with him. "OH SSSAY!" said Grandpa through his false teeth.

As the ensuing commotion died down, I began to piece the implications together. No maple syrup. No brightly wrapped presents. No chocolates, maybe. And then the strangest thing happened. I realized it didn't matter.

Christmas would come without maple syrup. Christmas would come without presents. Games would be played. Songs would be sung. Stories would be told. And, much more, Grandpa would be there. He had brought us the best gift of all: *himself.*

Of course, Grandpa wasn't taking it quite so well. As we climbed into the car, I heard him mutter, "Oh say." And I watched him reach for the cough syrup.

"Didn't you get anything at all?" asks Stephen.

"Yes, we did. But I don't remember much about the presents. I just remember Grandpa."

"Did he tell you lots of stories?"

"Yes. He especially loved to read us the Christmas story—of the Light that came blazing into the world, landing in a most unusual place, just for us. Of the Son of God, in a barn. And he told us that God could have given us anything

He wanted. But He gave us the best gift of all: *Himself.* That's what I hope you remember when you think of Christmas."

Above us, suspended from red string, is a row of Christmas cards. In the very center hangs my favorite:

> If our greatest need had been information,
> *God would have sent us an educator.*
>
> If our greatest need had been technology,
> *God would have sent us a scientist.*
>
> If our greatest need had been money,
> *God would have sent us an economist.*
>
> If our greatest need had been pleasure,
> *God would have sent us an entertainer.*
>
> But our greatest need was forgiveness,
> *so God sent us a Savior!*

In the glow of the Christmas tree, Rachael and Stephen sit quietly in wonder. "Tell it again, Daddy," they say.

Jeffrey sits quietly, looking at the stockings and wondering about something else. "What about we eat 'em," he says.

———

Every time we give, it's Christmas.

4
Fork in the Road

"THEY'RE DONE! HA! HA! ALL THE SCHOOL LUNCHES ARE DONE FOR THE NEXT 186 DAYS! NO MORE GETTING UP AT 6 A.M.! NO MORE MESSY SANDWICHES! NO MORE..."

" ────────────────────────────

The God to whom little boys say their prayers has a face very like their mother's.
                                                    —Sir James M. Barrie

My mother practices what I preach.
                                                    —A minister

I have three sons. Which one do you mean?
                                        —Hockey superstar
                                         Bobby Orr's mother
                                         when asked, "How is
                                         your son?"

The mother is the one supreme asset of the national life. She is more important, by far, than the successful statesman, or businessman, or artist, or scientist.
                                                    —Theodore Roosevelt

No one is poor who had a godly mother.
                                                    —Abraham Lincoln

──────────────────────────── **"**

I t has been one of those days. At 10:00 A.M., a computer blip swallowed half my morning's work and refused to give it back. At 11:30 a government official stopped by to examine my "To Do" pile and within five minutes had declared a national state of emergency. "What if that thing falls over?" he asked the building inspector. "I dunno," came the reply. "I suppose it could do serious damage." So they evacuated the entire building.

Okay, I'm exaggerating a little here, but the point is, I'm not having a good day. As the clock struggles toward 5:00 P.M., however, all that I've left unaccomplished is lost in visions of a quiet evening at home. Leaning back in my chair, I close my eyes.

Ramona will be waiting at the door when I arrive, her hair permed, her lips pursed. The children will be setting the table, smiles on their newly-washed faces. "No, Jeffrey," Stephen will be saying, "we're not supposed to eat the butter." "I'm sorry," his little brother will respond. "I was wrong. It won't happen again." The two will then exchange hugs. "Hi, Daddy," Rachael will say. "I didn't have time to wax the floor, but I'll do it after we eat." Dinner is roast beef. I'll surround mine with assorted vegetation and smother it in gravy. Following the roast beef, the children will beg to be put to bed early. "We want you and Mom to have some time alone," they will say. "You've probably had a tough day."

The drive home is a pleasant one.

As I park the car, however, I realize that something has gone desperately wrong. For one thing, half the neighborhood is in our yard. As I enter the house, I see the other half. They are raiding our refrigerator. Elsewhere in the kitchen my wife is halfway inside the dishwasher. The table is piled high with laundry, the floor with toys, and the stove holds not even a promise of supper. Setting down my briefcase, I fix my eyes on the oven. "So what's for supper? Roast beef?"

"Very funny," says Ramona, blowing hair from her sweaty forehead.

I sit down before the laundry. "So, what did *you* do today?"

Ramona stands up, brandishing a sharp fork. "What did *I* do today?" she asks, walking across the room—still holding the fork. "WHAT DID I DO TODAY?" She hands me a piece of paper—one which every homemaker should own—and stands by while I read it.

What I Did Today

3:21 A.M. — Woke up. Took Jeffrey to bathroom.
3:31 A.M. — Woke up. Took Jeffrey back to bed.
3:46 A.M. — Got you to quit snoring.
3:49 A.M. — Went to sleep.
5:11 A.M. — Woke up. Took Jeffrey to bathroom.
6:50 A.M. — Alarm went off. Mentally reviewed all I had to do today.
7:00 A.M. — Alarm went off.
7:10 A.M. — Alarm went off. Contemplated doing something violent to alarm clock.
7:19 A.M. — Got up. Got dressed. Warned Stephen.

7:21 A.M. — Made bed. Warned Stephen.

7:25 A.M. — Spanked Stephen. Held Stephen. Prayed with Stephen.

7:37 A.M. — Fed boys a breakfast consisting of Cheerios, orange juice, and something that resembled toast. Scolded Jeffrey for mixing them.

7:46 A.M. — Woke Rachael.

7:48 A.M. — Had devotions.

7:50 A.M. — Made Stephen's lunch. Tried to answer Jeffrey's question, "Why does God need people?" Warned Stephen.

8:01 A.M. — Woke Rachael.

8:02 A.M. — Started laundry.

8:03 A.M. — Took rocks out of washing machine.

8:04 A.M. — Started laundry.

8:13 A.M. — Planned grocery list. Tried to answer Jeffrey's question, "Why do we need God?"

8:29 A.M. — Woke Rachael.

8:30 A.M. — Helped Stephen with homework. Told him to remember his lunch.

8:31 A.M. — Sent Stephen to school.

8:32 A.M. — Had breakfast with Rachael. Porridge. Pulled toast out of VCR. Warned Jeffrey.

Rest of morning—Teacher phoned wondering why Stephen had no socks. Took them to him. Returned library books. Explained why a cover was missing. Mailed letters. Bought groceries. Shut TV off. Turned radio on. Heard report warning that there were "gale-force tornadoes in the area." Phoned Sherri about tornadoes. Planned birthday party. Ruth phoned wondering if I had heard about the sale on tomatoes in the arena. Phoned

Sherri and Julie. Told them I had heard wrong. Cleaned house. Wiped noses. Wiped windows. Wiped bottoms. Shut TV off. Teacher called wondering why Stephen had no lunch. Took it to him. Pulled spaghetti out of carpet. Cut bite marks off the cheese. Made funny-shaped sandwiches.

12:35 P.M. — Put wet clothes in dryer.

12:36 P.M. — Sat down to rest.

12:39 P.M. — Scolded Jeffrey. Helped him put clothes back in dryer.

12:45 P.M. — Agreed to babysit for a friend. Cut tree sap out of Rachael's hair. Regretted babysitting decision. Killed assorted insects. Read to the kids. Clipped ten fingernails. Sent kids outside. Unpacked groceries. Watered plants. Swept floor. Picked watermelon seeds off linoleum. Explained to Jeffrey why he shouldn't singe ants with magnifying glass. Read to the kids.

3:43 P.M. — Stephen came home. Warned Stephen.

3:46 P.M. — Put Band-Aids on knees. Organized task force to clean kitchen. Cleaned parts of house. Accepted appointment to local committee (secretary said, "We thought you would have extra time since you don't work"). Tried to answer Rachael's question, "Why are boys and girls different?" Listened to a zillion more questions. Answered a few. Cleaned out dishwasher. Briefly considered supper. Briefly considered heading for the hills.

5:21 P.M. — Husband came home looking for
food, quietness, romance.

I am finished reading now, but Ramona is still standing over me. Holding the fork. "Of course, not all my days go this smoothly," she says. "Any questions?"

"I'm sorry, Honey. I really am. Sometimes I get so caught up in my world that I forget how important yours is."

───────────

Often when Ramona and I are at public gatherings, she is asked the question: *Do you work?* I'm thankful she isn't holding a fork when this happens. Although she usually manages a kind response, I know she wishes she had the eloquence of the wife who once replied, "I am socializing two Homo sapiens in the dominant values of the Judeo-Christian tradition in order that they might be instruments for the transformation of the social order into the teleologically prescribed utopia inherent in the eschaton."

Then she would ask, "And what is it you do?" "I'm a lawyer" just isn't that overpowering then.

If you are a homemaker, let me encourage you: No one on earth can shape the mind of a child like his mother. It's true: Yours is the most powerful, most influential role on earth. I know the pay is poor, but the rewards are out of this world.

Now, I'd better go. I have to make supper.

═════════

*If you are called to be a mother,
don't stoop to be a queen.*

5
Journey into Trust

"DOES ANYBODY HAVE A ONE-INCH HEX NUT?!"

" ————————————————————————

Exit according to rule, first leg and then head. Remove high heels and synthetic stockings before evacuation: Open the door, take out the recovery line and throw it away.

> —Rumanian National
> Airlines emergency
> instructions

It's not that I'm afraid to die. I just don't want to be there when it happens.

> —Woody Allen

I know God will not give me anything I can't handle. I just wish that He didn't trust me so much.

> —Mother Teresa

I would rather walk with God in the dark than go alone in the light.

> —Mary Gardiner
> Brainard

God has never missed the runway through all the centuries of fearful fog.

> —Charles R. Swindoll

———————————————————————— **"**

Amerircan Airlines Flight 420. Blue sky. Early morning. Before me is takeoff. Beside me a beautiful blonde about my age. It hardly seems possible that we will spend the next few days alone. Hours ago we prayed with, kissed, and pulled the covers over three small children, leaving them in the care of friends.

"Welcome aboard, folks..." the captain is coming through more loudly than clearly as we taxi down the runway. *Shouldn't he be flying this thing?* I wonder as the wheels leave the ground. Apparently not. He is presently discussing the weather.

Now there's something you should understand: I'm not so good at flying. If you were up here, you'd know that. White knuckles. Nervous feet. If you were up here, you'd know why. For one thing, a smiling stewardess has just informed us that if we splash instead of crash, our seats can be used as flotation devices. I'd really like to know if this has ever brought comfort to a passenger. It's certainly not helping the 40ish gentleman across the aisle. He is consuming

45

liquor faster than the stewardess can supply it. "Keep the change," he says, eagerly twisting off another cap.

What bothers me most about flying (apart from the fact that scientists have yet to determine how metallic objects of this size and weight are able to get off the ground) is that none of us passengers can see the pilot. Oh, we can hear him all right, but how do we know he can be trusted? How do we know he hasn't just finished a fight with his wife? "Captain to tower. We're about to try out these flotation devices. Tell my wife it's all because of her...."

Yes, if I could just see the pilot, I would feel better. Reaching over, I take the hand of the blonde and close my eyes.

———

I'll never forget the day she broke the news. At the time it couldn't mean much to a love-struck teenager—merely another hazard of love down the road. But since her phone call that June day in 1980, the ever-present possibility has turned the years into a day-by-day journey into trust.

"There's a disease in my family," she said across the phone lines. "It's called Huntington's. I... I just wanted you to know that, before we get... well... any further along."

I could tell the words were difficult and I didn't know what to say. I only remember the strange feeling that grew in the pit of my stomach as she explained what it was.

"It's a genetic disorder that causes mental and physical deterioration." She paused, waiting for a reaction. There was only silence. "It's fatal," she continued. "Each of us kids has a 50-percent chance of getting it."

I did three things while she was talking: I listened. I prayed. And I realized I had better say something. "I'd like to marry you someday." My words were the last thing she expected. "I love you, Ramona."

Two years later, on a joyous rainy day, we became man and wife.

———

We are over Colorado now, experiencing what aviation people have chosen to call "turbulence." The 40ish gentleman is calling it something else. He is now in a horizontal position, dabbing clumsily at the spilled contents of a bottle of Coors Light. I find myself wondering what his life is like. Are beer stains on his pants the worst of his problems? Or is he just like me, wishing he could see the pilot, wondering what tomorrow will throw his way?

The turbulence worsens.

Ramona sits up and looks at me with an are-we-going-down-or-what's-the-deal? expression.

"Go back to sleep," I whisper, squeezing her hand. "It's going to be okay."

The turbulence has ended for now, and as we break through marshmallow clouds, a rainbow awaits.

Yes, it is going to be okay. Quite honestly, I don't always feel this way. But I know it is true. Because through sleepless nights His peace has been proof of His presence. And because I have the promise of One who hasn't broken one yet: "For I am the LORD, your God, who takes hold of your right hand and says to you, Do not fear; I will help you" (Isaiah 41:13).

Yes, the same hands that shaped the universe are forging my future. The same hands that were pinned to a Roman cross are holding mine.

It's hard to believe, but when your knuckles are white and you can't see the Pilot, it's worth hanging onto.

The mysteries are God's.
The promises are ours.

6
Out of Control

"MOM! I GOTTA GO TO THE BATHROOM!"

66 ————————————————————————

Is forbidden to steal towels, please. If you are not person to do such is please not to read notice.
> —Sign in Tokyo hotel

I have an obsession for detail. I like to make sure I cross my i's and dot my t's.
> —Unidentified job
> seeker on her
> application

Laughter is the closest thing to the grace of God.
> —Karl Barth

Ain't no sense worrying about things you got control over, 'cause if you got control over them, ain't no sense worrying. And there ain't no sense worrying about things you got no control over, 'cause if you got no control over them, ain't no sense worrying about them.
> —Mickey Rivers,
> former Yankee
> outfielder

Trust involves letting go and knowing God will catch you
> —James C. Dobson

———————————————————————— **99**

Our topic today is Embarrassing Moments. You know—those little complications that arise when you had something normal planned.

One of my favorite high-school teachers can identify. He used to interrupt perfectly good English classes with a crazed expression to remind us of the time he walked to the front of a huge auditorium for a short speech. "There's something the Lord has been driving home to me lately," he began as the capacity crowd leaned forward.

He paused for the sake of emphasis.

"I'll never forget it."

Silence.

"Uh, I'll never forget it."

Again silence.

He then backed slowly from the microphone, walked swiftly to his seat, and unceremoniously sat down. We high schoolers loved him for it.

But schoolteachers aren't the only ones with firsthand experience in this area. Church secretaries know all about embarrassment, too. On Wednesday they scurry about readying the church bulletin for the printer. On Sunday they sit in the back pew, right proud of their work until, two rows ahead, Mrs. Wilson nudges her husband, passes him the bulletin, and watches his face change color. The reasons are on page three:

> The church is offering a series entitled "The Church Explores the Issues." Tomorrow's lecture will be "Recycling—Our Garbage Is a Resource." There will be a potluck supper at 6 P.M.

> Last time we asked prayer for Jerry Butler's foot. After nine months of various treatments, it's finally all gone.

> Tonight's sermon: "What is Hell?"
> Come early and listen to our choir practice.*

Noah Webster showed remarkable restraint in defining embarrassment as "the state of being made self-conscious and uncomfortable." On paper it sounds fairly innocuous, doesn't it? But if Noah were to hang around our home long enough, he would change his tune. If Noah spent an entire evening at a Steve Green concert with our children, he would change his definition.

Since Noah died back in 1843, I realize we have a logistical problem here. But I'm still disappointed he wasn't there the other night when we unleashed our children on a rather large and unsuspecting audience of gospel music lovers. Of course Noah was not in attendance, but if he had been, his definition would now read:

> **em•bar•rass•ment** (im′•bar•ə•smənt) *n.* **1.** The result of taking Jeffrey Callaway to a concert. **2.** The result of sitting near Jeffrey's parents at the concert. **3.** To disconcert.

---

* These are actual bulletin excerpts.

Now you must understand that we didn't *have* to go to this concert. We could have spent a normal Thursday evening at home reading to the children or climbing walls with them. We had even considered a trip to the indoor waterslide (this my wife suggested before locking herself in the bathroom and laughing uncontrollably*). In the end, however, we opted for the concert. After all, we reasoned, the children would gain a new appreciation for the great songs of the faith. Besides, Steve controls a crowd so well, three young children would not be a problem.

It was nearing halftime when we realized we should have headed for the waterslide. Steve, in an act he had performed without a hitch a thousand times before, requested that the children join him at the front.

Proudly we watched ours file onto the platform with about 40 others. Proudly we watched four-year-old Jeffrey inform Mr. Green that "we have you on a movie." Rachael and Jeffrey even held hands as if they had rehearsed at home. You should have seen them: Their faces shining. Their blue eyes squinting as spotlights cast glorious halos about them. Ah, and my father heart was proud. *Hey, everybody, those are my kids! Our kids! The smiling ones. The ones with the halos.* Clearly this would be more relaxing than the Christmas program in which a three-year-old Rachael fanned the audience with her new red dress.

But relaxation was not on the program that evening.

As Mr. Green launched into the chorus "God loves a cheerful giver, Ha ha ha ha ha," he realized two things: the audience had joined him on the "Ha ha" part, and there were more "Ha has" than usual.

He also realized that MY SON was responsible.

You see, it had just become glaringly evident to all that Jeffrey had to use the facilities located at the rear of the building. In short, Jeffrey had to go.

---

* If you're wondering why, see my book *Honey, I Dunked the Kids* (Harvest House Publishers, 1993). Feel free to buy copies for friends, relatives, and even complete strangers.

As his parents frantically searched for the word EXIT, Jeffrey performed a little dance which is quite cute when kept to the family room but seldom performed at this type of concert. To the relief of all, the facilities were located in time, but not before the crowd was thrown into hysterics and Steve Green completely forgot his lines. (He would tell me later, "This was the first time I ever lost control of a concert." I would tell him, "You had him four minutes, Steve. We've had him four years.")

Upon arriving home that night, Ramona and I reflected on the events of the evening. And we realized again how many things are beyond our control. We may not like it, but it's true. It's true of our health. It's true of our future. And it's true, ultimately, of our children.

Then we did the strangest thing: We laughed until we couldn't stand up. It was the laughter of two who are learning to commit the things they can't control to the One who controls all things. Believe me, there's no better place to be.

Oh yes—you are probably wondering how Jeffrey is taking the whole thing. Well, his favorite video is no longer *Peter Pan.* It is Steve Green's *Hide 'Em in Your Heart, Volume Two.* Jeffrey now watches it with a grin that grows broader during "God Loves a Cheerful Giver." Perhaps he enjoys the music. Perhaps he enjoys the singer. Or perhaps he enjoys knowing that given the right situation, the right audience, and a big drink of water, he could upstage him.

You don't stop laughing when you grow old;
you grow old when you stop laughing.

7

Larry Norman, My Mother, and Me

❝ ─────────────────────────

One man's music is another's noise.
—Erwin Lutzer

Take an interest in your child's world and they may take an interest in yours.
—Steve Miller

Next to theology I give to music the highest place and honor.
—Martin Luther

The radiating influence from one person rightly related to God is incalculable.
—Oswald Chambers

Whom you would change, you must first love.
—Martin Luther King, Jr.

───────────────────── **❞**

It's Nostalgia Night at our house. Ramona and I have been going through some old record albums. Yes, records. You may remember them. A curious form of transmitting sound waves, but nonetheless very popular back when the earth was cooling and we were attending high school. Although we have since opted for compact disks, I still can't bring myself to toss out these old albums. Recorded here is a part of my past. A part of the good old days. A part of me.

Like today's teen, my friends and I found music very important, ranking it slightly ahead of eating and some days even ahead of girls. Stephen Rendall and I would purchase the latest contemporary Christian albums, rush them home, tape them, then insert them into our car tape decks. How we prided ourselves on those tape decks. Who cared about the car? We would gladly trade in all 6 cylinders on 100-watt speakers. For, you see, no mere machinery could move you like music.

I remember the day Stephen pulled up in his 1970

maroon Montego. Pinstripes. Whitewalls. Genuine imitation sheepskin seat covers.

"Climb in," he said, a grin connecting his ears.

I climbed in.

"Roll up your window."

I rolled it up.

Then, as we pulled away, he calmly inserted a Larry Norman tape, adjusted his sunglasses, and set the volume on 10.

Moments later our ears were pasted to the headrests with:

> I was lost and blind then a Friend of mine came
>   and took me by the hand.
> And He led me to His kingdom
>   that was in another land.
> Now my life has changed it's rearranged,
>   when I think of my past I feel so strange.
> Wowie zowie well He saved my soul,
>   He's the rock that doesn't roll.[1]

"STEVE," I yelled.

"WHAT?"

"THAT'S GREAT! ABSOLUTELY GREAT!"

He turned the volume way down to 5. "You're gonna be late for what?"

"No, I said that's GREAT. Turn it up."

Now you must understand that I was reared in a conservative community where such practices were frowned upon. Where Larry Norman was often confused with Led Zeppelin and the Beatles. This so-called Christian music was shallow, we were told, and, at best, would cause us to lose our hearing.

"Ha, impossible," we responded, before disguising our Imperials albums in George Beverly Shea jackets.

"Listen to this," I said to Dave Adkins as we huddled one afternoon near my brother Tim's stereo, hoping he wouldn't show up and murder us in cold blood for touching his stuff. Nervously, I dropped the needle on the latest from the Imperials:

> All we need is a little more time
> to get it together.
> There's a whole lot of people been tryin'
> to get it together.
> Like you and me—ooh ooh—that's all we need
> to be free,
> Just a little more time
> to get it together.[2]

"Wow," said Dave, "that George Beverly Shea's hot."

"And deep," said I. "Wow."

It was during these interesting days that I began playing music to another friend: my mother. Yes, you read it right. Almost every night I would invite her into my room and attempt to cross her eyes with the latest from Chuck Girard, Love Song, Phil Keaggy, The 2nd Chapter of Acts—even Petra. For some reason she always found time to pull up a chair and listen. I'm sure she rarely enjoyed my choices (just how much can a 55-year-old glean from "Lend an ear to a love song. Ooh ooh a love song. Let it take you, let it start"?), but she always cared enough to listen. And she encouraged me when she heard something praiseworthy.

Tonight, as I reminisce, I realize again how much greater is the influence of one who cares. One who takes time. For it is the truth: She who shrieks the loudest is not always heard the best. You see, while many of my friends heard only, "Turn it down, turn it off, or throw it out!" I was privileged to have a mother whose attitude was, "If he's going to listen, I'd like to know what he's listening to."

Sometimes I miss those days. The talks after the music died down. I think Mom does, too, although she probably doesn't miss the music that much—at least not as much as I miss my hearing.

———

An ounce of mother is worth
a pound of preacher.

66 ————————————————————————————

An archaeologist is the best husband any woman can have—the older she gets, the more interested he is in her.

—Agatha Christie

We should have marriage contracts. Five, 10, 15 years. It's this forever stuff that throws everything off.

—Jack Nicholson

Marriage is like a pair of scissors. You can't separate the parts. They move in different directions but whoever noses in between will be snipped.

—Harry J. Boyle

I'd trade my fortune for just one happy marriage.
—J. Paul Getty

A happy marriage is the union of two good forgivers.

—Robert Quillen

———————————————————————————— **99**

I'm an optimist when it comes to the institution of marriage. Oh, I know—like you, I've watched high fidelity go the way of the eight-track. And like you, I'm old enough to read the newspaper.

According to today's headlines, Glynn Wolfe and Linda Lou Essex are scheduled to exchange wedding vows this weekend. What will make it particularly meaningful for all in attendance, I'm sure, is the fact that it will be Glynn's twenty-eighth appearance at the altar and Linda Lou's twenty-third (for those who may be keeping score). The two are already listed in critical condition in the *Guinness Book of World Records*.

As I read their story, I try to imagine the potential complications clouding this weekend's ceremony:

> MINISTER: Wilt thou, Glynn, take this woman to be thy lawful wedded wife? Wilt thou love and comfort her until death do thee part... or until she singes thy waffles?
>
> GLYNN· Uh   ya, sure

MINISTER: Linda Lou, wilt thou forsake all others, keep thee only unto him, so long as ye both shall live...or until he starts watching the playoffs?

LINDA LOU: Sorry sir, you'll have to repeat that. I was distracted by a gentleman in the third row.

MINISTER: If anyone has reason that these two should not be joined, let him speak now or forever hold his peace.

CONGREGATION (rising): We do.

MINISTER: One at a time, please.

My first wife and I got to discussing Glynn and Linda Lou the other night. Of course I had a few observations immediately, not the least of which was, "Wow, I'll bet these people are really tired." You see, Ramona and I have been married 11 years now, so we've jumped our share of hurdles. But there are several reasons we would rather jump than stop running. There are some good reasons we remain in the race, eternally optimistic. Let me tell you about two of them....

————————

Victor Levi and Bernice Anne first exchanged shy glances at an August hot dog roast. He couldn't keep his eyes off her auburn hair, she his mischievous grin.

The year was 1939, and while the world went to war, they fell in love. Wisdom of the time said it was a dangerous move. After all, thousands of soldier boys were climbing aboard the war machine, never to return. But love rarely takes the safe road.

On a cold and snowy December day in 1942, they said their vows. A Canadian corporal on leave, and his 19-year-old bride: "I do take thee...for better, for worse; for richer, for poorer; in sickness and in health; to love and to cherish till death do us part."

Fifty years and five children later, the knot is still tied tight. Last night they sat on our sofa, surrounded by grand-children, talking of war, of peace, and of marriage.

"What made it last, Dad?" I asked, noticing he had moved a grandchild so he could hold Mom's hand.

He smiled and looked at her with that same old grin. "Senility," he said. "I wake up each morning and I can't remember who this old girl is. So each day is a new adventure."

"No, I'm serious. Give us five good reasons you're still together." It was an unusual pop quiz, complicated somewhat by three grandchildren clamoring for their attention.

"I'll tell you what," said Mom, removing our youngest son's index finger from her ear, "give us a little time. I'll write them out for you."

The next morning she handed me a note. "You won't show this to anyone, will you?" she asked. "I don't want people to think it's the final word on marriage."

I simply smiled, "You know me, Mom. I wouldn't dream of it."

Five Reasons We're Still Together
by Victor and Bernice Callaway

1. *Example.* When we were married, we hardly knew about divorce. We didn't know any divorced people. I guess everyone at our wedding, including us, fully expected the knot to stay tied. We had watched their marriages. We had seen their faithfulness. We would stay faithful, too. We realize you won't have that advantage, son. Some of your closest friends may pack it in. But no matter how dark the road gets, you will find bright examples of faithfulness. And when you can't find examples, you can still *be* one.

2. *Commitment.* Sometimes I felt like walking out on Dad. And a few times I did! Early in our marriage I

occasionally took long walks to get away from him. But I always returned to his loving arms. We made a pledge before God that we would stay committed to each other for life. You may have heard of the golden anniversary party that was thrown for an elderly couple like us. The husband was quite moved by the occasion and wanted to tell his wife just how he felt about her. She was very hard-of-hearing, though, and often misunderstood what he said. While family and friends gathered around, he toasted her: "My dear wife, after 50 years I've found you tried and true." Everyone smiled their approval, but his wife said, "Eh?" He repeated louder, "AFTER 50 YEARS I'VE FOUND YOU TRIED AND TRUE!" His wife shot back, "Well, let me tell YOU something—after 50 years I'm tired of you, too!" It's a funny story, but remember that commitment doesn't need to be like that. Marriage is not a life sentence, it is a joyful privilege. But to know the full extent of that joy you must remain committed to each other through the tough times—and we've had our share.

3. *Bible reading and prayer.* Through reading God's Word and praying together almost every night, we learned what God planned and expected for our marriage. We memorized verses that encouraged us to be loving, kind, honest, and to keep on forgiving. We asked God for guidance and He provided it. We prayed for children and embraced each one of them as gifts from God.

4. *Togetherness.* As a Christian family we stuck together, warts and all. Though we often failed, we learned (and are still learning) to admit wrong and ask for forgiveness. We laughed lots. We cried lots. We talked lots. We worked together and we played together.

5. *Goals.* Since the day we said our vows, our goal has been to walk worthy of the Lord and to keep on walking until we see His face. Sometimes we have fallen flat on *our* faces, but we've been given grace to get up and claim the promise, "My Presence will go with you, and I will give you rest."[1]

Aging brings with it a whole new challenge. It is no flat plateau; sometimes the hills seem steeper and the cliffs more precarious, but we are learning to trust God for what is ahead and to thank Him for the abundant and undeserved mercies of the past.

You probably won't read about Mom and Dad in your morning paper (they make pretty dull headlines next to Glynn and Linda Lou) and you certainly won't find them in the *Guinness Book of World Records* (unless they have opened a new category for "Most Time Spent Babysitting the Grandchildren Without Compensation"), but when I get discouraged about the state of marriage today, I like to think of two young lovers who stood at the altar as the temperature dipped to 45 below.

They knew that ten days later the soldier boy would go back to war, leaving his tearful bride waving from a train station platform. And so they joined hands and promised to be faithful.

They had no idea that their second child would die in their arms or that they would spend their entire lives below the poverty line. But they vowed to comfort each other no matter what came their way.

By today's standards Mom and Dad didn't have much. Just $75, a solitary wedding ring, and a suitcase full of dreams. Half a century later, they still don't have much. Just a little old mobile home and a car that sometimes runs. But their dreams were never about good fortune. Instead they dreamed of children who would love the Lord—and they got five of them. Instead they dreamed of years of faithfulness—and they got 50 of them. You can travel the world, but I'll guarantee you one thing: You will never meet two wealthier people.

———————

By the way, Mom did give me permission to reprint the note. And as she did, she reminded me of a few final clichés: "Even when you are 70 you have to work at marriage" and, "It's never over till it's over." Then she said with a twinkle in her eyes, "I think we're pretty safe, though. Dad may be senile, but I've grown too old to run away from him."

══════════

Marriage halves our griefs, doubles our joys,
and quadruples our expenses.

9

The Trouble with Genesis

"COME ON, DAD! YOU'RE THE ONE WHO'S ALWAYS TELLING ME TO PRACTICE WHAT I READ IN THE BIBLE!"

" ———————————————————————

*It ain't those parts of the Bible that I can't
understand that bother me, it is the parts that
I do understand.*

—Mark Twain

*It is very difficult indeed for a man or for a boy
who knows the Scriptures ever to get away from
it. It follows him like the memory of his mother.*

—Woodrow Wilson

*Impression without expression leads to
depression.*

—Howard Hendricks

*A Bible that's falling apart probably belongs to
someone who isn't.*

—Christian Johnson

——————————————————————— **"**

We've had to lay down the law at our house: No more Bible reading before 6:00 A.M. That's right, it was getting out of hand. I first realized we might have a problem the night I was reading Dr. Seuss to the children. Stephen, who was five at the time, interrupted the story (of a one-feathered bird's envy of a two-feathered bird) to explain, "That's not 'Gertrude McBuzz,' Dad, that's 'Gertrude *McFuzz.*'" His younger brother and sister didn't care either way, so long as the narration did not badly contradict the illustrations, but Stephen's biggest concern was the spelling of a bird's maiden name. As a discerning father, I immediately recognized that the boy is a perfectionist, a characteristic which is superseded only by his determination to *be* one.

The problem worsened as he entered school, journeying past Dick and Jane and into grade two where they string words together into actual sentences. One day not long ago he rushed home carrying a library book on dinosaurs. Opening to page one, he began to read: "Fifty...um...billion...years ago..."

"I'll tell you what," I said with astonishing wisdom, "you read the book of Genesis and I'll buy you a new pair of ice skates." He looked up from his book. "Ice skates?"

"Yes, ice skates. Size two." That evening he went to bed without being threatened and began to read aloud: "In... the... um... beginning... God... created... the... heavens... and... the... um... earth." *Ah, I thought to myself, my wallet is safe. After all, the boy is seven. Genesis is 50 chapters. At this rate he will finish sometime during his sophomore year of college. What good will size two ice skates be then?*

A few hours later I fell asleep, entertaining nostalgic dreams of the time my father (who is partly Scottish) talked me into reading the New Testament. The reward was a coveted digital watch, and, upon finishing Revelation, I showed up to claim the prize. "Aha," said Dad, turning the dream into a nightmare, "You read it in English, didn't you. I told you to read the original Greek."

The nightmare is interrupted by a seven-year-old standing at the foot of my bed holding a big red *Illustrated Children's Bible* and smiling proudly. "Daddy, guess what? I'm on chapter six!"

"Uh... that's really good, Stephen. What time is it?" Turning my head I am confronted with the awful truth: It is 4:03 A.M. Mountain Standard Time. "What in the world? ... Stephen, you go back to bed and go to sleep."

The child obeys—or at least partly. He goes to bed, but not to sleep. By the time I enter his room at 6:30 he has been on a cruise with Noah, a mountain with Abraham, breathed the sulfur of Sodom and Gomorrah, and learned all he will need to know about circumcision. As I sit down beside him he is zeroing in on chapter 25. "Dad, what's a Hittite?"

The next morning is much the same. By 4:00 Jacob has stolen Esau's blessing. By 5:00 Joseph's wicked brothers have sold him to Egypt. By 6:00 they have been forgiven—and by 7:00 Stephen is as miserable a little boy as you will meet. "Jeffrey, you stole my Lego!" he hollers, waking me from slumber. Then I am greeted with the sounds of him pounding on his little brother. "You give it back!" Jeffrey screams a response and the fight is on. "It's mine!... No it ain't!... It's mine!"

Normally, as the first rays of morning sneak through our blind and gently usher in a new day, I like to spend a few minutes quietly considering the opportunities which lie ahead; thanking God for a lovely rest, a new start, another chance to serve Him. This morning all I can think of is sulfur. *"He's been reading about divine judgment, Lord. I'll illustrate it for him."* Hurrying down the hall, I command Stephen into my study. "Bring the spoon," I thunder, causing Jeffrey to scurry under a blanket.

Before using the spoon, I have made it a habit over the years to take a few moments to relax. To simmer down. To put things in perspective. To practice my stroke. Sometimes these moments are *very* few, but today they are many. Why? Because, as I hold a small boy on my lap, I realize that it is tough to spank someone when you are partners in crime. You see, ever since I was old enough to read I have found the Bible fascinating. But I have always found it easier to enjoy God's Word as literature than to let it change my life. I've read Jesus' words, "Love your neighbor as yourself" and, just like Stephen, I've pounded on those around me. Not with my fists, but worse: with my words. With my gossip. I'm still learning that there is no virtue in reading about Abraham's obedience. I must obey. There is no virtue in studying Jesus' words. I must put them into practice. A verse somewhere in the book of James comes to mind: "Do not merely listen to the word, and so deceive yourselves. Do what it says."[1]

"Stephen, you're tired. I want you to say sorry to Jeffrey, then get some sleep."

"Are you gonna spank me?"

"No. But I want you to do something. I want you to remember that the most miserable people I know are the ones who can tell you all about the Bible without obeying it.

I'm glad to see you reading God's words, but that isn't enough. You must let them change you."

The following Monday, he received his ice skates. And I also bought two bookmarks. One for him and one for me. They are covered with panda bears and the verses: "Love the Lord your God with all your heart and with all your soul and with all your mind... and love your neighbor as yourself."[2] By Friday, Stephen was using his to mark his spot—in Leviticus.

———

Obedience is the key to freedom.

10

Once upon a Toothache

"WELL, THIS IS A FIRST! I NEVER HAD A PATIENT SWALLOW ONE OF MY GLOVES BEFORE!"

"

God whispers to us in our pleasures, speaks in our conscience, but shouts in our pains: it is his megaphone to rouse a deaf world.
—C.S. Lewis

In Italy for 30 years under the Borgias, they had warfare, terror, murder, bloodshed—but they produced Michelangelo, Leonardo da Vinci, and the Renaissance. In Switzerland, they have brotherly love, 500 years of democracy and peace, and what did that produce? The cuckoo clock.

—Graham Greene

An unexpected vacancy for a knife-thrower's assistant. Rehearsals start immediately.
—Classified ad

What do people mean when they say, "I am not afraid of God because I know He is good?" Have they never even been to a dentist?
—C.S. Lewis

Adam ate the apple and our teeth still ache.
—Hungarian proverb

"

In the springtime of my fourteenth year, I experienced the hazards of tooth decay. In those days my mother baked potatoes by encasing them in tinfoil, setting the oven to 350, and leaving the potatoes to sizzle for one hour or until the desired tenderness was achieved. This she measured by forking the potato dead-center and watching the steam rise. The method seemed to work, but for one small problem: the fork left behind small shards of tinfoil, which were a nuisance to eaters and a dreadful torment to bad teeth. I experienced that torment one day after our family had gathered for a quiet dinner.

If you've ever had your ears pierced by someone whose aim was bad, you know the feeling.... "AAAIIIEEE!" I screamed, holding the side of my head.

"You don't like the food, Son?" asked Mom.

"AAAIIIEEE!" I replied.

"I believe it's his tooth," said Dad with great discernment. "I'll call the dentist first thing in the morning."

I think it appropriate to note here that my father was, in

most instances, a compassionate, rational man. But the next day he set aside these virtues, strapped me into our blue 1965 Pontiac, and pulled up before a red brick building on main street. Silver letters graced the front: Harold's Dental Clinic, Ltd. We children knew it by another name: Harold's House of Horrors.

Once inside, I was coaxed away from my father, down a gloomy hallway, and into The Chair. Moments later, Dr. Harold Pullman, D.D.S., arrived, bringing to mind the words my brothers had shared with me the previous night—as darkness descended. According to them, Dr. Pullman was once addicted to laughing gas but had given that up in favor of alcohol. He now drank "like a fish" and was often "under the influence" while on duty. When confronted, he admitted the problem but assured those concerned that he drilled less accurately when sober, so the matter was still working its way to Town Council.

With the memories came an acute desire to leave The Chair, but by then Dr. Pullman stood over me, wielding a sharp stainless steel instrument the size of a lamppost. "Open wide," he said as his assistant trained a spotlight into my eyes. "Hand me the D764 with the Honed Hook." He held out his hand, accepted the instrument, then began to probe.

"So, Philip, you've been experiencing some discomfort lately?"

"Yauush," I replied.

"Is it this one?"

"Nooo."

"This one?"

"Nooo."

"This one?"

"YAAAUUUSSSHHHH!"

"It's abscessed," said Dr. Pullman, peeling me carefully off the stuccoed ceiling. "Looks like we will need to do a root canal." The pain had dulled my hearing. All I could hear was, "Roof panel" and, "Let's amputate!"

Pushing myself out of The Chair, I yelled: "DAAAAD!"

Two decades have passed, but I still remember that amputation. Pain, it seems, is the one experience we humans relish only in retrospect. If you doubt me, just attend a parents' party on any given night. The ladies sit quietly on couches, while the guys stand by the table swirling ice cubes and wondering what their wives are saying about them. In reality, they are not discussing husbandry at all. They're swapping scars.

> JULIE: My water broke 14 days before Joel was born.
>
> ROSALIE: No kidding. I thought Benno would never come. The labor lasted 23 hours.
>
> SHARON: I was 23 *DAYS* with our oldest! Then they took her by C-Section!
>
> RUTH: I don't remember a thing. They drugged me. I woke up when TJ was in third grade.

Meanwhile, the guys are discussing less violent events. Like football.

Stephen, our seven-year-old, had his first baked-potato experience tonight. Actually, he bit into an ice cube, which left a tooth hanging like a loose shingle from the roof of his mouth. What to do? If I leave it in, it may work loose while he sleeps, causing a major problem. If I take it out, well, how can I—without losing a finger? The parenting manuals don't cover this.

"Why don't you join the tooth and a doorknob with some fishing line?" suggests my wife before scurrying from the room. "Then slam the door."

"Pardon me?"

She backpedals, then pokes her head around the corner. "My dad did that and it worked."

"He slammed the door on your head?"

"No, no. I stood in the corner and he slammed the door. My tooth hit the wall."

"What?"

"Never mind. I'll get the stuff."

The stuff is a little tube of gel that freezes what it touches. I apply some to Stephen's gum and he immediately goes into orbit (this was not one of the side effects listed on the box). Apparently the pain has crept into his mind.

An hour passes and we are no closer to the goal. At last I hold his head firmly and say, "We will just have to leave it in there."

"Noooo."

As he hollers, I insert my thumb and push. The tooth breaks free. Stephen looks at me in horror, cups the tooth in both hands, and laughs with tears streaming down his face.

———————

"Daddy, why do we have to hurt?" It is well past bedtime now but Stephen can't sleep. The tooth under his pillow will turn into a dollar before morning, but he wants more for his trouble.

"That's a good question, Son."

As his tongue darts in and out of the gap in his mouth, I search for an answer. How do you explain to a seven-year-old that the world is a cruel place and life is not fair? How do you explain that pain will come? That sometimes it will make way for a new tooth or a new baby, but just as often it will leave you strapped into The Chair with a spotlight in your eyes.

The only thing that comes to mind is the story of my own amputation by Harold Pullman, D.D.S. So I tell him. He listens, mechanically flicking his tongue and smiling.

"You know, Stephen, one day our pain will be only a memory. The Bible tells us that God is preparing a place for us. When we get there, He will wipe every tear from our eyes. There will be no more death or crying or pain. You think about that the next time you bite an ice cube."

"Okay."

"Now, you really need to get some sleep. Goodnight, Son."

"Goodnight." The boy looks braver now. "Dad? How did he pull the tooth?"

"With a big silver thing."

"Did it hurt?"

"Yes. It hurt."

"Dad...um... I have two more of 'em."

"Two more of what?"

"Teeth. Loose ones."

"We'll look at 'em tomorrow, okay?"

"Ya," he says, through the hole in his smile. "Tomorrow."

———

We cannot grow without pain.

" ────────────────────────────

How immense appear to us the sins that we have not committed.
> —Madame Necker

Grace is love that cares and stoops and rescues.
> —John R.W. Stott

There but for the grace of God, goes John Bradford.

> —John Bradford upon seeing a condemned man

──────────────────────────── **"**

One hot summer night when I was tucked safely in bed, our shed went missing. The vacancy left a large black square on our lawn and mysterious whispers sweeping the neighborhood. According to my parents, there was no mystery at all. The previous inhabitants of our house had merely taken what was rightfully theirs—but my brother Dan believed differently. He claimed the shed was stolen by a band of wandering gypsies and that we'd best saddle up our bicycles and go in search of them. The more I considered the black square, however, the more I realized that something else could have happened. Something bizarre and sinister. Something an imaginative ten-year-old could use to his advantage somewhere down the road.

When you are born and raised in the buckle of the Bible Belt and the worst thing you've done is pick Mrs. Pike's forbidden raspberries, people like Lester Schwartz present a problem.

Mr. Schwartz blew through our Christian school most Septembers with the most amazing personal testimony I had ever heard. A former felon with real tattoos, his life had been marred by immorality, occult practice—even murder.* But then the day came when he fell to his knees on the cold cement of a prison cell and was gloriously transformed by God. We children listened wide-eared from the edges of our chapel pews as the story unfolded, and as it drew to a close, we applauded. It was the loudest response I had heard since the missionary from North Africa held up a black mamba skin which a cluster of second-grade girls thought to be alive.

During the following weeks, the story came up often in schoolyard discussions and the following September the excitement increased with the nearness of Mr. Schwartz's return. Finally, the day arrived. "We have a special guest this morning," said the school secretary, Miss Hale, who stood no taller than she sat. "Some of you may remember him from last year, but let's give him a warm Alberta welcome just the same." The older kids whispered to the younger ones and both clapped eagerly. Mr. Schwartz stood, dwarfing Miss Hale, who sat down and pulled out a hanky.

"You may have heard my story before," he began, rolling up his sleeves, "but I think it bears repeatin'. I don't tell you this 'cuz I'm proud of it, yuh understand; I just hope I can save some of you little 'uns the troubles I been through."

As I listened to his story for the second time, a curious feeling came over me. It was envy, pure and simple. You see, I had no testimony at all. I would have killed for his, but mine wasn't worth telling. At the tender age of five, Jesus came into my heart. My mother knelt with me by my Styrofoam bed as I asked Him to cleanse me of things like pinching my

---

* Years later I learned that there was some discussion as to whether or not a person should be allowed to speak of such vices in Friday morning chapel. Our school secretary Miss Hale felt that children should keep their minds on "whatsoever things are pure," but the principal noted that the Bible didn't gloss over people's problems, and neither should we. "To be forewarned is to be forearmed," he said. So Lester was issued an open invitation to return.

sister, stealing raspberries, and not liking Sundays. *How can God use a testimony like that?* I asked myself. And so, as the others listened to Lester, I invented a new one. It was the best testimony a ten-year-old could think of, and two weeks later I arrived at our Friday Sing-and-Share Chapel ready to deliver.

We had just finished the second stanza of "Pass It On" when Miss Hale stood, I think. "Does anyone have something to share?" she asked. I waited an agonizing two or three seconds, then got to my feet, quickly reviewing what I had rehearsed. "I'm not proud of this," I planned to say, while folding my hands and looking my schoolmates in the eyes, "but this summer I blew $100,000 that I made dealing drugs." Gasps would surround me. Miss Hale would haul out the hanky. Maybe faint. But I would continue undaunted: "Oh, I know it sounds like a lot for a kid who's only ten and lives just up the hill, but I fell in with the wrong crowd.

"It all started the day Juan Gomez drove slowly by our house, eyeing the shed where we kept our rabbits, Fudge and Marshmallow. Stopping his Cadillac, Juan removed his sunglasses and motioned me off the swing set. 'Hey,' he said, holding up a wad of twenties, 'you wanna buy lots of gum?'

"The temptation was too great for me and before I knew it I was sneaking out at night to fly with Juan by Lear Jet between Colombia and our baseball field. We stashed the drugs in our shed along with large piles of money and I was back in bed before the sun was up.

"One day, Fudge and Marshmallow started acting weird. Dad said it looked like they were from another planet or something, not human rabbits at all. The next morning, I was reading in my personal devotions where it says that all of us have sinned and come short of the glory of God and I came under conviction. I asked God's forgiveness right then and there, and I knew I would have to do something about the shed. So that night I let the rabbits go and stuffed the shed with sticks of dynamite that I had bought at Vaughn's Hardware. Then I lit a long fuse and climbed into bed. Some of you may remember the bang."

At this point, Miss Hale would probably blow her nose and I would have to wait while she regained some composure. Then I would continue. "Juan came by the next day with his sunglasses on. He couldn't find the shed. But he did find two black rabbits running in funny circles on some charcoal, and my Daddy and me arm in arm, surveying the damage. That was the last I saw of Juan. He didn't stay around to find out what happened. But my father knew everything. I told him. And when I did, he hugged me and said that I had learned some valuable lessons: that I should choose my friends carefully and that money will eventually go up in smoke. Then we knelt on the charcoal and prayed."

The story had come together quite nicely in my mind and I was thinking an altar call would be a real possibility—when suddenly I realized that my sister Ruth had come to chapel that day. The sister I had pinched. The one who knew about my summer, who knew it wasn't like that.

"Did you have something to say, Philip?" asked Miss Hale.

"Who, me? Uh...I...um...just wanted to say that I had a good summer." And I sat down.

———

Three or four years passed before I worked up the courage to confess my imaginings to my father. When I did, he smiled a lot, then said some things that I've mostly forgotten. But I do remember these words: "Sometimes little boys whose worst crimes were committed in raspberry patches are the toughest criminals of all." At the time I didn't know what he meant, but I'm starting to understand. You see, it's easy to go through life looking at the gaping wounds of those around us. We will find plenty of them these days. But too often those people who focus on the sins of others miss their own. "Every one of us is a sinner," Dad said, "no matter how dull or exciting our testimony." The Bible says it best: "It is by grace you have been saved, through faith—and this not from yourselves, it is the gift of God—not by works, so that no one can boast."[1]

When we kneel before God one day and hear Him welcome us home, it won't be because of what we did or did not do. It will be His grace. Nothing more. Nothing less. Nothing else.

The more I think about it, the more I realize it's the most amazing story of them all.

———

Sin rules, until grace dethrones it.

12
Sins of Summer

EVENTUALLY, ALAN CAVED IN TO
PEER PRESSURE AND SMOKED
THE SNEAKER.

" ———————————————————————————

We find the defendants incredibly guilty.
> —Verdict given in Mel
> Brooks' *The Producers*

If you plant for a year, plant rice; if you plant for a decade, plant trees; if you plant for a century, plant people.
> —Robert McClure,
> medical missionary

Take my advice, dear boys...shun...bad company and cigarettes. Don't do anything, boys, you are afraid to let your mother know.
> —Ernest Cashel,
> murderer hanged in
> 1904

My mother had a great deal of trouble with me, but I think she enjoyed it.
> —Mark Twain

God does make us better if we are honest about being sick.
> —Steve Brown

——————————————————————————— **"**

Ah, summertime. The very word brings back memories, doesn't it? Memories of bare feet. Of sleep-overs. Of fishing trips. Memories of lying to strangers about your interest in the environment. Uh, wait a minute, I'm getting ahead of myself there. Allow me to explain. . . .

It was the summer of my tenth birthday when my friend Gary and I established The Gang of Two. Early each morning after our fathers went to work, we borrowed their shovels and spent the day burrowing deep into the bowels of the earth. I, Captain Phil, pretty much gave orders. Private Gary pretty much followed them.

Each day—thanks in large part to Gary's unwavering obedience—we burrowed a little deeper. Each day, by 5:00 P.M., we returned the shovels to their rightful spots. And no one was the wiser.

As July became August, The Fort became home. Dead tree branches camouflaged her from the onslaught of rival gangs. Tall weeds concealed her inhabitants from passersby. In those weeds we sat, decked out in imaginary khaki outfits, imaginary guns in hand, launching surprise attacks on passing cars, which were Nazi U-boats and sometimes tanks.

Then one morning in mid-August, after dying theatrically from a U-boat torpedo, Gary spoke the fatal words: "I'm bored."

As captain, it was my job to turn such words into adventure, so I quickly responded, "What say we stop saving The Fort and start saving The Earth." The thought was a new one for both of us, which was why Gary pushed aside two large flowered weeds, looked at me with his head to one side, and said, "Huh?"

It was a good question. After all, neither of us could spell Greenpeace. But there in the tall weeds atop our fort we discussed, for the first time in known history, recycling.

That afternoon, as the hot summer sun beat down through the ozone layer and danced on the asphalt around our feet, we put our plan to work: We purged main street of every visible cigarette butt.

> GARY (picking up another one): "Boy, are these ever disgusting!"
>
> ME (loudly, in the direction of the curious passersby): "YES, GARY. PUT THEM IN THE BAG. THEN WE'LL THROW THEM IN THE TRASH."
>
> GARY (with a loathing look): "To think people actually smoke these things!"

Upon completion of our task, we carried the butts to our headquarters in the woods and concluded The Plan: we smoked what remained, one by one. Right down to the filters.

In fact, we recycled pretty much anything we could get our lips around that summer. Tea leaves. Cinnamon. Dried dandelions. Pencil shavings. Newspaper. Cardboard. You name it, we sat in the weeds and inhaled it.

I believe it was a Wednesday that changed our lives. Gary approached me on his bicycle, breathless. "You ain't agonna believe this," he said, throwing himself on the grass, rolling in the suspense of it all.

"Okay, let me guess. Um, it's gotta be candy. Your mom bought you all you can eat?"

"No, better."

"Uh, she bought you a motorcycle?"

"Nope," he said, unable to contain his excitement any longer. "I found A PACK OF 'EM. It ain't even been opened."

"Naw, you're lyin'."

But he wasn't lyin'. In fact, carefully concealed in the tall shadow of an obscure telephone pole was proof: Player's Filter Tip, unopened and beckoning.

Casting anxious glances in all directions, we stripped off the plastic and divided The Pack evenly. Ten apiece. And we smoked them. Every one. Right down to the filters.

As our time behind the pole drew to a close, we pooled our wisdom and experience, noting what scientists would later discover: Anything that tastes this bad can't be too good for you. Or, as Gary put it so eloquently, "These things are awful. Let's never ever touch another one as long as we both shall live." After shaking tobacco-stained hands on it, I suggested, somewhat deliriously, that we get home and, furthermore, that we do so quickly, maximizing the time needed to reenter the nonsmoking zone.

"Hmmmm," sniffed Gary's mother. "What's that smell?"

Half an hour had passed and she was standing outside the family restroom, wondering who had established a tobacco plantation on her property without securing permission. Gary crouched in the bathtub, caught yellow-handed. "I, uh, was smoking," was all he could say.

But I was older than Gary. I was wiser. I knew that as ye smoke, so shall ye reek. So, in an effort to keep the consequences of my own sins at bay, I slipped silently through our back door and up to the medicine cabinet. From there I tiptoed to my room, concealing a can of spray deodorant and a full tube of toothpaste. After lengthy attention to personal hygiene, I was finally able to approach my parents. "Hmmmm," sniffed my father. "You sure smell nice, Philip."

Later that evening I crawled into bed, a satisfied smile stuck to my face. *Boy, are you ever brilliant,* I thought. *No one will ever know.*

Mom entered my room then, opened the window, and sat on the bed. "Did it taste good?" she grinned.

"Uh...whaa...supper? Oh, yes, Mom. It was very good. Thank you."

"When I was a girl," she continued, "I tried smoking my dad's pipe. I didn't like it.... How about you?"

"Me neither, Mom."

She could have spanked me then. Or quoted Scripture. She could have reminded me that nothing we do will ever be hidden from God. That no amount of toothpaste or deodorant will cover our sins. That they really will find us out. She could have reminded me that the story doesn't end there. That because of what Jesus did on the cross we don't have to hide. That because He took our sins we can approach God, forever forgiven.

Instead, she leaned over and kissed me squarely on the forehead.

"I'll never smoke again," I said. Then, "Mom, how did you know?"

She grinned again. "Well, son, sometimes ten-year-old boys forget that their mothers have friends, too."

From the bathroom came the sound of my dad's voice: "Hey, has anyone seen the toothpaste?"

———

Wise parents never lose their child's heart.

13

Throwing in the Towel

HOCKEY IN HEAVEN

"

JANE HATHAWAY: Chief, haven't you ever heard of the saying, "It's not whether you win or lose, it's how you play the game"?

MR. DRYSDALE: Yes, I've heard it. And I consider it one of the most ridiculous statements ever made.

—From "The Beverly Hillbillies"

Losing is the great American sin.

—John R. Tunis

I don't even let my daughter beat me at Tic-Tac-Toe.

—Bob Gibson, Hall of Fame pitcher

Success consists of getting up more times than you fall.

—Oliver Goldsmith

The juggler comes closest to our hearts when he misses the ball.

—Richard J. Needham

"

My friends to the south sometimes ask why Canada is relatively crime-free, while they are left to languish in concrete jungles such as New York, Miami, and Billings, Montana. The answer, I believe, has little to do with our judicial system, our public policy, or even the fact that our igloos are spaced very far apart. Instead, it has everything to do with hockey.

You see, while the streets of Detroit, Los Angeles, and Boston are crawling with criminals, we Canadians can roam the streets unarmed at any hour for one simple reason: Our potential muggers are either playing hockey or watching it.

For those of you who know little about the sport and so have yet to experience the joy of watching friends sign the casts on both of your legs, allow me to provide a little background. The word *hockey* finds its origins in a combination of the North American Indian word *tamahakee,* or "to chase with great speed," and *splochet,* French for "to bludgeon." It is a team sport played on a slippery surface with sharp blades, sharp sticks, a dangerous projectile called a puck, and not nearly enough padding. It is also the only legitimate sport since Roman rule which permits its participants to shishkebab opponents and, if caught, be made to spend two short minutes in a penalty box thinking about doing it again.

I was only three when my older brothers, in their finite wisdom, saw fit to introduce me to the sport. I had no idea what they were getting me into. I had no idea that my nose would be broken three times, that I would be knocked cuckoo seven times, and that a doctor would be employed full-time to stitch my face. Okay, I'm exaggerating there. I was knocked out only once.

By tenth grade I had spent hundreds of hours on the ice. Practicing, practicing, practicing. It will come as no surprise to you that my reasoning was simple: *If I practice enough,* I thought, *one day I will do something heroic. One day I will score a goal so big I'll forget the broken nose, the stitches, and the uh...the uh...oh yes, the time I hit my head.*

That same year my dream looked like it might keep its promise. Laying aside all individual goals, our team members became a cohesive unit, confused the critics, and fearlessly shishkebabbed our way to the championship game. So, on a Saturday night in late March, the crowd (which consisted almost solely of teenage girls) packed our small arena to watch the stars come out. Peering in nervous awe through a crack in the locker-room door, I had the distinct feeling that this would be *my* night. The night of the big goal. Yes, the years of practice were about to pay off.

But as the game progressed, the dream began to fade. In fact, as the clock ran down to the final minute, the dream had all the makings of a nightmare. We were behind 3-2.

Then, in a moment I'm sure someone somewhere still remembers, I took a pass from the corner and rifled the puck past a sprawling goalie. The girls went wild. The game was tied. And I was a hero—at least for the moment.

When overtime began, I had the distinct feeling that destiny was on my side. Call it premonition; call it intuition; call it ridiculous; for a late adolescent it was very real. Tonight would be *my* night and I knew it. Then, sure enough, about five minutes into overtime I had my chance and I seized it. It is a moment which is forever available to me on instant replay and sometimes in slow motion. As the puck slid toward the open net, I dove, trying desperately to forge its destination. As the crowd rose to its feet, I swatted the puck across the goal line. The girls went wild. So did my opponents' mothers. But they weren't cheering for me. You see, I had just scored INTO MY OWN NET.

I don't remember much else then. I do remember making a beeline for the locker room, where I sat down and threw a white towel over my head. And I recall the comments: "That's okay, ya done your best, man" and, "Don't worry about it, eh? Anyone in this room coulda done that... if he was totally uncoordinated."

Through the muffled laughter, I determined to hang up my skates for good.

Upon arriving home that night, I headed straight for my room. A bad case of the flu had kept Dad from the game. I didn't want to make him sicker by telling him about my big goal. Maybe in three or four years he would be well enough to deal with the details. But Dad entered my room, and I told him everything. I didn't dare look at his face. I could only stare at his red plaid housecoat.

When I finished, there was silence for a minute. Then he put his hand on my knee and began to laugh. I joined him. It was the last thing either of us expected. It was the very best thing.

You see, Dad was letting me know that my worth was in no way associated with winning a game. His message was crystal clear: "No matter what happens, I love you."

Wise is the father who understands that shaping a life is more important than winning a game. Wise is the parent who knows that the biggest victories are seldom posted on a scoreboard.

Eighteen years have passed since the night Dad and I laughed together. I still remember it as the night I determined to skate again. In fact, I'm still skating. I've even scored a few goals over the years—in the right net. But none has been as memorable as that overtime goal, a lifelong reminder that the biggest victories can be found in the ruins of defeat. A lifelong reminder of my heavenly Father's unfailing love.

Hey, when you can't even remember how many times you've hit your head, you don't take such lessons lightly.

———————

*Our mistakes provide greater opportunities
than our successes.*

14
Of Big Things and Small Packages

UNFORTUNATELY, THE TEDDY BEAR THAT BOB RESCUED FROM THE MIDST OF I-90 BELONGED TO SOMEONE ELSE'S FIVE-YEAR-OLD.

" ──────────────────────────────

I never cease to amaze myself. I say this humbly.
　　　　　　　　—Don King, boxing
　　　　　　　　　promoter

*If ever a man becomes proud, let him remember
that a mosquito preceded him in the divine order
of creation.*

　　　　　　　　　—The Talmud

*It's ludicrous for any Christian to believe that he
or she is the worthy object of public worship; it
would be like the donkey carrying Jesus into
Jerusalem believing the crowds were cheering and
laying down their garments for him.*

　　　　　　　　—Charles Colson

*He has achieved success who has lived well,
laughed often, and loved much.*

　　　　　　　　　—Bessie Anderson
　　　　　　　　　Stanley

────────────────────────── **"**

Daytime television affords limitless opportunities to discover what is *really* going on in the world. My wife is finding this out as she scans the channels, remote control in hand. First up we have Phil Donahue. Phil is excited about today's program. And with good reason: He will be interviewing aliens who are suing the *National Enquirer.* Sally Jesse Raphael is enthusiastic, too. Her first guest is a psychologist known to cure people who snore in four-part harmony. And let's not forget Geraldo. Before the hour is up, he will be pinned between some angry animal rights activists and zookeepers who use liposuction.

Thankfully, Ramona rarely watches TV. But today is different. Today she is scanning the channels looking for me.

A few months ago I was asked to appear on "Just for Parents," a nationwide family program that seeks to provide an alternative for parents who are weary of aliens inhabiting their living rooms. Of course, I accepted. But I was nervous about appearing on television. I mean, let's face it, some people are born with a complexion for radio. Besides, what if they ask you an important question such as, "Phil, what are the seven key ingredients to a happy home?" and all you can think of is, "Now I lay me down to sleep, I pray Thee Lord my soul to keep"?

When I begin telling friends, however, I realize that I am not so much nervous as I am proud. After all, none of them have been on TV, except for Harold Leo, who saw himself once while walking by Radio Shack. *Wow, Phil. You're really something,* a voice seems to whisper. *You're going to be on television.* And the whisper pleases my ears.

"Daddy?" Rachael, who should be sleeping, has just tip-toed into my study to say goodnight. Again.

"What are ya doing?" she asks, holding down the "z" key on my computer. An important paragraph is swirling through my head and I don't have time for questions.

"I'm writing, Rachael. You are supposed to be in bed."

"Will you play with us tomorrow?"

"No, I have to go away for a few days."

"How long will you be gone?"

"Three sleeps."

"Will you be lonely?"

"I will miss you, Rachael. Goodnight."

The next day as I pack my suitcase, Jeffrey brings me his stuffed bear. Much of the fur has been loved off. The eyes are not positioned for seeing. But it is Jeffrey's favorite animal. "You might be lonely," he says, handing it to me. "You shall take Heide Bear."

Airline passengers watch from the corners of their eyes as I take my seat. A grown man with a briefcase and a teddy bear. Hang on to the children, Ethel. He looks unstable. Insecure. Probably needs counseling. They are right. All that's going through my mind is, "Now I lay me down to sleep." I can't even remember the next line.

On the day of the program, Ramona gathers the children to watch. Jeffrey shows special interest: "Daddy has my bear," he says proudly. And, sure enough, there it is. On national television. The hosts jokingly try to pry it away from me, but I hang on. "My four-year-old was concerned that I would be lonely," I tell the cameras, "so he gave me his bear."

Jeffrey is excited about his dad being on TV. So excited that he manages to sit still for almost two minutes—watching Bear. Then he saunters off down the hallway to build swords with which to poke his big brother.

————————

In the darkness of a Sunday morning I leave the hotel and travel to the airport. It's early, but I'm smiling. Who wouldn't smile? The weekend was a success. I appeared on one of the top-rated morning shows in the country. I spoke several times, made lots of contacts, sold lots of books. I have even received invitations to return. As the plane takes off, the voice is no longer whispering. It's hollering in my ear: *You're pretty important, Phil.* And I believe it.

Then, suddenly, the awful truth hits me: Fellow passengers aren't watching me from the corners of their eyes. They are not questioning my sanity. I have my briefcase, but no bear. It is lying on the floor of a hotel room.

As we take off, images flash through my mind. The day my first book was published. After receiving copies in the mail, I proudly rushed it home to show the kids. Rachael held my life's work in her hands and smiled at the cover. Then she set the book down and, looking out the window at the bird feeder, asked, "Dad, what kind of sparrow is that?" Jeffrey was more interested, though. He picked up the book and chewed on a corner.

A few months later I walked to the stage in front of a large gathering to receive a few awards. Stephen was there. He was sitting near the back, and I hoped he could see me. He would be proud, you know. But later I learned that he had been too busy playing Mr. Squishhead with a friend to even notice. They were squeezing their faces at each other, oblivious to my moment in the spotlight.

Woody Allen's *Murder in Manhattan* is showing on a large screen at the front of the plane. I try to watch but the image is blurry. I can't see past the tears. "Lord," I pray, "I've been so caught up with myself lately that I've left some things on the floor. I've been too busy working to play with the kids. Too busy writing to read Your Word. Too busy talking about myself to hear Your voice. Please forgive me."

———

At home, the children wait. When I walk through the door Rachael greets me with three days' worth of hugs. Stephen wants to show me a castle he has been working on.

Jeffrey just wants his bear.

I sit him down beside the phone and start my confession. When I finish, he begins to cry. "You help me dial," I say. 1...9...he is wiping away the tears and poking at the digits...6...4... "Hello?...Yes...could I talk with the manager?...Hi...I stayed there this weekend and left a small brown bear in my room....Huh?...You're kidding. ...You're not kidding?...Great....Here's my address...."

A broad smile crosses my face as I hang up the phone. "Guess what? The lady had your bear on her desk. She's going to put it in a box and mail it to us in the morning."

Jeffrey thinks it's Christmas.

———

A week later the package arrived. And now, whenever I travel, its contents come along. A four-year-old boy insists. In fact, I'm writing this chapter in a strange hotel room, but a friendly animal sits atop my briefcase. Its eyesight has worsened. More fur has been loved off. But I wouldn't trade this bear for anything. Oh sure, I receive some strange stares when I board airplanes. And Ethel still rounds up the kids. But I carry with me a small reminder that all the success in the world doesn't compare to the trust of a child. A reminder that those who pursue big dreams must be careful not to leave the little ones behind.

———

Success is like perfume.
It may be sniffed, but never taken internally.

15

Charles Atlas and The Secret Formula

"HIS HIGH SCHOOL REUNION IS TOMORROW."

" ————————————————————————————

He is richest who is content with the least.
————Socrates

Why be under-sized? Use Dillow's Lengthening Compound! Guaranteed to increase the height one foot for each six months' use.
————1914 advertisement
for Dillow-Hahn

I look dorky in all my films.
————Harrison Ford,
movie star

We are so vain that we even care for the opinion of those we don't care for.
————Maria Ebner-
Eschenbach

If the value of an article is dependent upon the price paid for it, Christ's death made our value skyrocket. Let no one say we are worthless. God is not a foolish speculator; He would never invest in worthless property.
————Erwin Lutzer

———————————————————————————— **"**

Willie Major was barely ten when he willed me his entire estate. It consisted solely of an Archie comic-book collection, but as far as I was concerned it was pure gold. I'm still not sure why he did it. Perhaps he noticed how much I enjoyed reading them. Perhaps it was out of deep appreciation for our longtime friendship, or it may have had something to do with the way I threatened him with a slingshot.

Whatever the case, I enjoyed his comic books. Oh, I didn't care much for the Archie part, but I loved the ads. To be specific, the Charles Atlas ads. You may remember: Mr. Muscle is reclining on the beach surrounded by adoring women, when lo and behold, Mr. Certified Wimp comes along and accidentally kicks sand in his face. This causes Mr. Muscle no small degree of agitation, which he alleviates by taking hold of Mr. Wimp and smacking him into another time zone.

` While there, however, Mr. Wimp is told about The Secret Formula. If he pays enough money and follows enough instructions—*presto*—he will be free to kick as much sand as he wants and perhaps pull freight trains with his teeth. Of course he pays the money, follows the instructions, and soon grows larger than Mr. Muscle. He then returns to the beach and finds his foe still reclining there, still surrounded by adoring women.

"Hey," says Mr. Former Wimp standing over an astonished Mr. Muscle, "I believe that's my beach towel."

"Is not."

"Is so."

The dialogue continues this way until Mr. Muscle is chased into another zip code. One where there are no adoring women and no one has heard of The Secret Formula.

It didn't take long for me to identify with one of the characters. I was Mr. Certified Wimp. When I was only five my older brother Tim told me so. According to a legend of his making, I was born on a hot July evening, weighing in at roughly 6 pounds, 38 inches. Though to this day my mother vehemently denies the whole thing, Tim assured me with much nodding of his head that the legend was historically true. He went on to tell his astonished baby brother that the nurses had never seen anything quite like me and that the doctor just stood there during the delivery, wide-eyed and whistling.

After lengthy deliberation with various hospital staff, the doctor finally handed me to my exhausted mother and proclaimed, "Well, Mrs. Callaway, it's a looooong story, but we think you may have given birth to a hot dog."

"Timothy Wray Callaway!" chided my mother. "Don't you say such things. Philip is just right. He is fearfully and wonderfully made."

"Ya," said Tim before being banished to his room. "Fearfully."

Although I never fell for the legend, the coming of fourth grade showed me that, at least in part, the tale was true. This was the year I first discovered girls. "Wow!" I said to myself during a moment of extraordinary enlightenment, "girls are different!" To show my deep affection for them, I did what all normal fourth-grade boys do: I began pulling their pigtails.

"You're skinny," said a mean, freckled girl after I finally let go of her red hair. "You're so skinny you have to wear skis in the bathtub to keep from going down the drain."

I was shocked. "Oh yah?" I retorted. "Well, you're so fat that...um...that you have to turn sideways to...um... keep from catching a cold." My words left us both a little bewildered.

It sounds funny now, but when I got home from school that day, I cried.

In eighth grade our class executive decided to celebrate the ending of the school year with a swimming party. I was horrified. How would I cover my legs, arms, and chest with a one-piece swimming suit? I had tried before. It didn't work. In fact, I couldn't even keep a Speedo in its rightful spot—without suspenders.

And so, a month before our party, I dug out an old Archie comic book and ordered up The Secret Formula.

Upon its arrival, I eagerly tore open the package. *Time is short,* I thought, *this had better be instant.* Inside were drawings of an extremely muscular man doing exercises. That was it. No drink. No clever little formula. Just a work-out list accompanied by illustrations of some guy who had muscles in places where I didn't even have places. Undaunted, I descended to our basement and began the Charles Atlas Gaunt to Gargantuan Health and Nutrition Plan. During the next two weeks those instructions were followed religiously: I did push-ups with my feet on a chair. I did sit-ups with my legs in the air. I did chin-ups, leg-lifts, wrist-rolls, knee-jerks. You name 'em, I did 'em. A thousand times over.

The night before school was dismissed, the class executive—in its infinite wisdom—canceled the swimming party.

Throughout my high-school years, however, I continued the program. I was determined that if ever they announced another swimming party, I could recline unashamedly on a beach towel. Even if they had to carry me there—in a pine box. You know what? The formula didn't work. Oh, I suppose I learned a few things about discipline, but I must tell you, I'm almost as skinny today as the day I opened that package. In fact, I still can't force the scales past 156 without carry-on luggage. Believe me, I've tried everything else.

The funny thing is, I really don't mind. The turning point came the day I discovered that Charles Atlas didn't have The Secret Formula after all. David did. I was reading the book of Psalms when his words hit me:

> For you created my inmost being; you knit me together in my mother's womb. I praise you because I am fearfully and wonderfully made; your works are wonderful, I know that full well. My frame was not hidden from you when I was made in the secret place. When I was woven together in the depths of the earth, your eyes saw my unformed body. All the days ordained for me were written in your book before one of them came to be.[1]

I read it again. And again. Then I memorized it. And today when I gaze into a full-length mirror, I remember those verses and I smile from ear to ear. Not because I'm able to chase anyone from the beach. Not because I'm overwhelmed by my attractiveness. But because the One who spoke the stars into space called my name. Because the One who crafted the mountains and hollowed out the ocean depths left His fingerprints all over me. Because God Himself would rather die than live without me.

Tonight, I think we'll celebrate. I think we'll pile the kids into the car and go out for ice cream. And then we'll go swimming. I'll try to remember to throw in some suspenders.

———

Those unhappy with what they have
will never be happy with what they want.

" ————————————————————————

*Life is an onion. You peel it off one layer at a
time, and sometimes you weep.*
—Carl Sandburg

*The school of hard knocks is an accelerated
curriculum.*
—Menander

*I have no understanding of a long-faced Christian.
If God is anything, He must be joy.*
—Joe E. Brown

*We cannot truly face life until we have learned to
face the fact that it will be taken away from us.*
—Billy Graham

———————————————————————— **"**

"**T**ell me, what has been the biggest surprise of your life?"

The question was asked by the host of a Chicago talk show. It was directed towards me. My answer? "Uh...my biggest surprise, sir? I think it's your question."

Now that I've had time to think it over, I would rephrase that slightly. I could easily mention our children. You see, we had them about as rapidly as modern bionics will allow. Just how fast, you ask? Well, the way my wife tells it, the anesthetic from the first birth was still working quite well during the third.

A friend wanted to know what it's like to have three kids in three years. I told him Ramona and I are far more satisfied than the guy with three million dollars.

"How so?"

"Well, the guy with three million wants more."

Seriously, each of our three has been a delight. To watch them grow. To witness the development of their spiritual gifts. Take Jeffrey, for instance. He's only four, but already he's exercising the gift of encouragement. Just the other day he was talking to a former friend of ours who has been struggling with her waistline. By her own admission she has been sneaking from fridge to fridge. From diet to diet. Apparently Jeffrey sensed her discouragement and determined to practice his gift in a most practical way. "Um," he said, "did you know that dinosaurs were even bigger than you are?" And you wondered why I called her a *former* friend.

Yes, children have brought us our share of surprises. But if I was asked about the biggest surprise of my life, I wouldn't talk about the kids.

Maybe I would sift through my filing cabinet. It's full of interesting little clippings on various subjects. Let's see... Premillennialism... Quicksand... Rapture... ah ha, here we are: Surprise. The file isn't that thick, but here at the front are some absentee notices sent by creative parents and received by surprised teachers.

> I kept Monica at home today because she was not feeling too bright.

> Please excuse Paul from school yesterday. He had a stomach egg.

> The basement of our house got flooded where the children sleep so they had to be evaporated.

My father could also tell you all about surprises. He got one the other day when he arrived at our door and was greeted with those tender words every grandparent loves to hear: "Hi, do you have any peppermints?" As Stephen and Grandpa sat on the couch chewing on some, Stephen was asked, "What would you like to be when you grow up?"

The seven-year-old wrinkled his eyebrows and thought for a minute. "I'd like to play drums in a rock band," he said. "Like Petra."

After my 72-year-old father picked himself up off the

carpet and got his eyes uncrossed, he said, "Could Grandma and I come watch you?"

"Nope," responded Stephen, without skipping a beat, "you'll be dead."

————

"What has been the biggest surprise of your life?"

I suppose if Dad were on that talk show in Chicago, he would have no trouble answering the question. And now that I've had a little time to think it over, I would have no trouble either. I would tell the following true story:

It began in March of last year with a phone call home.

"I've got great news," I told my wife. Then I proceeded to read from the front page of the newspaper: "The gene that causes Huntington's disease has been discovered after a decade-long search, sparking hope that a cure can be found for the deadly neurological disorder."

Ramona listened, her heart pounding.

As a young teen she was told that her father had the disease before he died in a drowning accident. The news meant there was a 50-50 chance she would eventually die from it.

During the next 20 years, she watched three siblings— all in their 30s—contract the disease, one making the slow and humiliating journey to a nursing home.

By the time the newspaper clipping arrived, Ramona had resigned herself to the fact that she had it, too.

The symptoms were there: depression, lack of sleep, loss of memory, irritability, occasional clumsiness—even a craving for sweets. I kept telling her that each of these could be traced to living with me. This she found amusing for awhile, but every time she stumbled, every time she arrived at the fridge and forgot why she was there, she knew she had Huntington's. So each time *I* stubbed my toe, I told her about it. Each time *I* arrived at the fridge and stared blankly at the salad dressing (a daily occurrence), I would inform her. And we would laugh. And sometimes we'd cry.

With the morning paper came the realization that for the first time in history those who were at risk could know their future with a simple blood test.

So two months later we sat together in a cold, sterile laboratory as a nurse took Ramona's blood. Normally I'm not so eager to watch the procedure, but I wanted to make sure they got it right. "There's no chance of the tubes getting mixed up, is there?" I asked, wondering how many times she had heard that one. The nurse smiled at my worry, then showed us how the tubes were labeled. I appreciated the method. But I had no idea that limited public interest and even less government funding would make us wait ten months for the results.

During those months we were surprised by the comfort of God's promises. On the countless nights when we lay in bed unable to sleep, Bible verses hidden away in my childhood came back to comfort us.

> God is our refuge and strength, an ever present help in trouble. Therefore we will not fear, though the earth give way and the mountains fall into the heart of the sea.[1]

> "For I know the plans I have for you," declares the LORD, "... plans to give you hope and a future."[2]

> In all these things we are more than conquerors through him who loved us. For I am convinced that neither death nor life, neither angels nor demons, neither the present nor the future, nor any powers, neither height nor depth, nor anything else in all creation, will be able to separate us from the love of God that is in Christ Jesus our Lord.[3]

> When you pass through the waters, I will be with you; and when you pass through the rivers, they will not sweep over you.[4]

Peace I leave with you; my peace I give you. I
do not give to you as the world gives. Do not let
your hearts be troubled and do not be afraid.[5]

When I had run out of Bible verses, I would look over at
Ramona. She was usually asleep. And, almost without
exception, she was smiling.

———————

In early January the phone call came.
The waiting was over.
The verdict was in.
We would hear it—on February 14. Valentine's Day. *Was
this someone's idea of a cruel joke?* I wondered. *This is a day
for Cupids and hearts . . . not final verdicts.* Then I realized
how fitting it was. You see, when I stood at the front of a
church on August 28, 1982, I said I would be her sweetheart
no matter what came our way. In sickness and in health.
Until death separated us. I had little idea what that meant,
but it is a promise I will not break. And I renewed my vow
again as we entered the waiting room on Valentine's Day.

Another couple joined us. My brother Tim, too. He's a
mature pastor, you know. He told funny stories while we
waited. Perhaps that sounds strange. Insensitive. Even irrev-
erent. But we had done all the crying. We had spent ten
months on our knees. And so, in the face of certain tears, we
did some first-class laughing.

Tim had just reached another punch line when the doctor arrived looking a little bewildered. People don't laugh in
this waiting room.

We wound our way down a corridor and into a dimly lit
office. Beside an oak desk sat another doctor. No one is
smiling, I noticed. We exchanged nervous greetings. She
opened an envelope, examined its contents, and kindly said,
"Ramona, you have the normal gene."

A thousand things flashed through my mind during the
next few seconds. *She has the disease. The normal Huntington's gene. Our children have a 50-50 chance of the same.*

In ten years the girl I love will be an invalid. Then the doctor said, "Which means you don't have Huntington's."

There was silence.

"You mean I DON'T have it?" Ramona was on the edge of her chair.

"You don't have it."

"I DON'T?" She was standing now.

"You *don't.*"

Next thing we knew we were hugging two doctors and thanking them profusely. We were lost in a hallway and we didn't mind at all.

You know, when I think of happiness, I think of that moment. Who wouldn't rejoice at such news? Who wouldn't celebrate the removal of a 20-year death sentence?

But if I were asked today about the biggest surprise of my first 32 years on the planet Earth, I wouldn't talk about happiness. I'd talk about *joy.* You see, the last ten months could not be described as happy. But strangely, they were jam-packed with joy. Joy doesn't depend on happy endings. On good news or sunny circumstances. Joy comes from knowing that whatever happens, God is good. Whatever happens, God loves me. Whatever happens, we will live forever because of the death sentence God placed on His Son.

Oh yes, you're wondering about Ramona's symptoms. Well, the doctors attribute them to depression, but she is smiling a little more lately. And she finally admits that most of them can be traced to living with me. I'm wondering, though, about the craving for pickles and ice cream.

===

God offers us joy.
Don't settle for the pursuit of happiness.

Peter, Paul, and Barry

AFTER THE TEAM LOST 20 CONSECUTIVE GAMES, COACH FARNSWORTH DID HIS BEST TO HELP HIS PLAYERS REGAIN THEIR CONFIDENCE.

" ———————————————————————

A failure is a person who has blundered but is not able to cash in on the experience.

—Elbert G. Hubbard

Not the power to remember, but its very opposite, the power to forget, is a necessary condition for our existence.

—Sholem Asch

God doesn't always use those who please Him. He uses whoever He pleases.

—Michael Card

The real legacy of my life was my biggest failure— that I was an ex-convict. My greatest humiliation—being sent to prison—was the beginning of God's greatest use of my life; He chose the one experience in which I could not glory for His glory.

—Charles Colson

——————————————————————— **"**

I always loved playing baseball with the big guys. When I stepped up to bat, I knew they would have mercy on me. Pitchers who ordinarily threw lightning would lob the ball in a gentle arch. My knees would knock. My hands would tremble. My swing would be no-where near the ball. On occasion, though, the bat and ball would intersect, causing quite a commotion in the infield. But usually by the sixth or seventh swing Larry Charter was jumping up and down on his glove and yelling, "He's out! He's out!" Then Danny Boutwell, who was larger than Larry and downright imposing when glaring from the pitcher's mound, would smile and wave me back into the batter's box. "He's allowed another strike," Danny would say. And he would lob another pitch. My hands would still tremble. My knees would still knock. But this time I would smack one—just over Larry's head.

Ah, I loved playing baseball with the big guys.

I spoke recently on "What My Parents Did Right." Afterwards, a man who couldn't have been more than 40 approached me. His name tag said *Barry.* "I enjoyed your talk," he said, "but when I hear of 50-year marriages I want to crawl someplace and hide. I'm on my third one, Phil. Where do I go from here?" My response probably wasn't the best, but it was all that came to mind: "God can forgive you of yesterday and He will help you be faithful today." Barry had tears in his eyes. "I feel like a failure," he said, and walked away.

———————

I wish I could talk to Barry again. I would tell him about John Creasey. In his bid to have a book published, John received 753 rejection slips. Yes, 753. He could have wallpapered his home, but John's mind wasn't on interior decorating. Instead, he sent out one more manuscript. The result? The English novelist went on to publish 564 books.

I wish I could tell Barry about Babe Ruth. You see, most sports trivia buffs can tell you that The Babe hit 714 home runs. But few know that he struck out 1,330 times.

Most of all, I would like to tell Barry that the Bible is full of stories of saints who struck out. I would tell him about Peter, the disciple who vowed to follow Jesus at any cost then denied Him with an oath. I would tell him about David, the king who was guilty of adultery and murder then referred to as a man after God's own heart. Why? Because, like Peter, David knew where to go with his failure. When the prophet Nathan confronted him about his sin, David prayed, "Have mercy on me, O God, according to your unfailing love; according to your great compassion blot out my transgressions. Wash away all my iniquity and cleanse me from my sin. . . . Create in me a pure heart, O God, and renew a steadfast spirit within me. Do not cast me from your presence or take your Holy Spirit from me. Restore to me the joy of your salvation and grant me a willing spirit, to sustain me."[1]

"Failure doesn't come in the falling," David would tell you. "It comes in not getting back up."

———————

In the 1992 Summer Olympics, British runner Derek Redmon tore a ligament midway through his race. As the rest of the runners went on to finish, Derek lay on the ground holding his leg and writhing in pain. For years he had pushed himself toward the goal: Olympic gold. For years he had focused all his energy on one thing: winning. Now those hopes and dreams lay shattered on the track.

Then, amazingly, as television cameras rolled, Derek pushed himself off the ground. As the crowd watched, Derek began to run again, determined to finish the race. But after a few short strides his legs buckled and he slowed to a walk.

A man appeared on the track then. Security guards tried to stop him, but he was as determined as the runner. Putting his arm around Derek's shoulder, he began coaxing him along. As the crowd thundered its approval, the two crossed the finish line.

The man was Derek's father.

———————

If you are reading this, Barry, I hope you'll remember Derek. And I hope you'll remember the words of the apostle Paul: "One thing I do: Forgetting what is behind and straining toward what is ahead, I press on toward the goal to win the prize for which God has called me heavenward in Christ Jesus."[2]

Have your knees buckled lately? Are your dreams lying in a shattered heap on the track? Perhaps you feel like a little kid standing at home plate, wondering who is counting the strikes. Never forget: God is there with you. He towers above the rest, offering forgiveness and a steady hand. With His help you can knock this next pitch clean out of the ballpark.

———

Fall seven times, stand up eight.

The Last Laugh

Earlier tonight I walked alone to a small house on the corner of Third Street and Ninth Avenue. It seemed strange, securing permission to be there.

When I was a boy, I owned the place. I skipped its sidewalks, climbed its trees, slid its hallways. We dubbed it The White House then, because...well...because it was white. Today the paint is gray. The new owner may change its colors again, I'm told, but for me it will always be white.

Twenty-five years ago, the house was home. It was also enormous. The ceiling was out of reach without the help of my dad's shoulders. The hallway stretched on into forever, particularly at midnight. Now I can reach the ceiling with no trouble, and the hall lasts only six strides.

If I stand still and listen real hard, I can hear the voice of my brother Dan in the backyard, announcing baseball pitch by pitch. It's the bottom of the ninth and there are two outs. Babe Ruth is at the plate pointing toward the left-field bleachers. *It's a long fly ball... it's going... it's going... it's gone.* One day Dan hopes to be on real radio, calling real games, but for now he is content to dream.

In the front, my sister Ruth pulls our Little Red Wagon. Her dolls are passengers. They sit lopsided, blanketed but uncomfortable. She can't wait to have real dolls. I hope she is kinder to them.

In the living room, my brother Tim is holding a crusade, a Bible in one hand, a finger on his text: John 3:16. In a few minutes he will give an altar call and we will come forward. He won't quit humming "Just As I Am" until we do.

Stepping outside, I sit on the patio. Much has happened since I sat here last. Much has changed. Twenty-five years ago I thought everyone had a mom and dad who loved each other. I thought everyone had older brothers who would sit on their tiny chests and big sisters on whom they could squeal. Of course, it didn't take me long to discover that this is not the case. That happy homes are not the rule. That four strong walls are not enough to fend off tragedy. That happy endings are too often the stuff of fairy tales.

Across the road, the skating rink where I thought I fell in love is now a parking lot. The baseball diamond where I beaned Mark Silver with a curveball is just a field. Over by that stump Stevie Graham talked me into eating a whole onion. The stump was a tree then, its branches strong. They held me as I climbed to hide the tears. Stevie called some friends, and I climbed higher. The tree is gone, but the tears are making a comeback. I must be getting old; I'm 32 and already I'm nostalgic.

The backyard is neatly groomed now. When I was a boy we wore a hole in the center by June, with soccer balls and bare feet. The neighbor kids helped us. I heard Mom say once that she didn't mind. "I'd rather have my kids than grass any day," was how she put it. Grass would always grow, but children would grow and be gone. She didn't know how soon.

At home, Jeffrey is waiting. "I can't sleep," he says. What is it about four-year-olds? This afternoon his mother couldn't keep him awake; now I can't pay him to go to sleep. Together we head for the rocking chair.

Jeffrey sits on my lap now, examining my forehead, gazing at the wrinkles. "Daddy," he says, "how old are you?"

"I'm 32, Jeffrey."

"You have cracks in your head," he says. I have been told this before, but not by one so young.

In the stillness of midnight, I hold him tight to my chest. And I laugh. These days will soon be gone, I know, but for now I will enjoy them. "Lord," I pray out loud, "help me hold tightly to the things that last. The family You have given me. The Word of God. My relationship with You. Help me let go of the things that fade away."

"Amen," says Jeffrey, smiling.

I laugh again. He will forget a whole lot of things. But I hope he remembers my laugh.

PS: Dan went on to be a radio broadcaster. I listened to him this morning. Ruth has four children of her own. Real ones. She is kind to them. And Tim? Well, he's a preacher. His church board hired an organist, so he doesn't need to hum.

If you would like to send the author your comments or interesting accounts of life in your home, write:

Phil Callaway
P.O. Box 4576
Three Hills
Alberta, Canada
T0M 2N0

Notes

Chapter 7—Larry Norman, My Mother, and Me
1. Larry Norman, "The Rock that Doesn't Roll."
2. F. Allen "Smokey" Roberds, "Time to Get It Together." Used by gracious permission of the songwriter (in exchange for an autographed copy of *Daddy, I Blew Up the Shed* and an autographed copy of the coveted Imperials album "Time to Get It Together").

Chapter 8—Fit to Be Tired
1. Exodus 33:14

Chapter 9—The Trouble with Genesis
1. James 1:22
2. Matthew 22:37,39

Chapter 11—Daddy, I Blew Up the Shed
1. Ephesians 2:8,9

Chapter 12—Charles Atlas and The Secret Formula
1. Psalm 139:13-16

Chapter 16—The Biggest Surprise of My Life
1. Psalm 46:1,2
2. Jeremiah 29:11
3. Romans 8:37-39
4. Isaiah 43:2
5. John 14:27

Chapter 17—Peter, Paul, and Barry
1. Psalm 51:1,2,10-12
2. Philippians 3:13,14

Honey, I Dunked the Kids!

is a delightful collection of tales from the bright side of family life. Phil Callaway's tender and some-times hilarious family memories bring laughter and encouragement to anyone involved with kids—especially parents! Illustrated by nationally syndi-cated cartoonist John McPherson, *Honey, I Dunked the Kids* accents the positive values of family life in short, fun-to-read stories.

Other Good Harvest House Reading

365 THINGS EVERY COUPLE SHOULD KNOW
by *Doug Fields*

This little book is loaded with lighthearted wisdom and insight into the hallowed (and often harried) institution of marriage. *Don't yell at each other unless the house is on fire* is just one of the witty, poignant exhortations you and your partner can enjoy together. These maxims will spark fun, romance, and care in your relationship!

365 THINGS EVERY MAN SHOULD KNOW
by *Doug Fields*

Every man should know dirty socks left on the floor cannot walk to the hamper on their own is just one of the many fun and thought-provoking proverbs of manly wisdom you'll find in *365 Things Every Man Should Know.* Tongue-in-cheek wit and sage advice join forces in this lighthearted look at men and manhood.

365 THINGS EVERY WOMAN SHOULD KNOW
by *Doug Fields*

There are just certain things a woman should know, and certain things that *only* a woman *can* know. These gems of insight, witty sayings and pithy one-liners will have you thinking *and* laughing at the same time!

365 THINGS EVERY PARENT SHOULD KNOW
by *Doug Fields*

So your kids didn't come with instructions? Don't worry. These bite-size bits of lighthearted wisdom will encourage you every day of the year. They're funny. They're pointed. And they're packed with dynamite advice for raising great kids.

I STOLE GOD FROM GOODY TWO-SHOES
by *Heather Harpham*

For four years Heather has been writing stories that tickle the funny bone while showing God's surprisingly personal involvement in our everyday lives. Readers of *Virtue* and women from all walks of life will smile and laugh—and then pause to ponder as Heather reaches into the "plain vanilla" events of life and draws out the very thing that can make the ordinary *extraordinary*. This a perfect gift for mothers, daughters, and friends—anybody who enjoys humor and insightful writing.